fear is POWER

fear is
POWER

Anthony Gunn

Hardie Grant Books

This book is dedicated to my beautiful wife, Mel. Thank you for all your love and support.

Published in 2006
by Hardie Grant Books
85 High Street
Prahran, Victoria
3181, Australia
www.hardiegrant.com.au

National Library of Australia Cataloguing-in-Publication Data:
    Gunn, Anthony, 1975– .
    Fear is power.
    Bibliography.
    ISBN 1 74066 408 6.
    1. Fear. 2. Anxiety. 3. Psychology, Applied – Popular
    works. I. Title.
152.46

Cover and text design by Nada Backovic
Cover photography courtesy Photolibrary
Typeset by Lynne Hamilton, Prowling Tiger Press
Printed and bound in Australia by Griffin Press

Every effort has been made to incorporate correct information and to attribute copyright. The publishers regret any errors and omissions and invite readers to contribute up-to-date or additional information to Hardie Grant Books.

10 9 8 7 6 5 4 3 2 1

Contents

PREFACE

When I was a kid, my father was a teacher at the local high school, which mightn't have been so bad if the cane wasn't in use back then. After receiving their punishments, the local boys would look for my brothers and me to exact revenge. That was when we took up boxing.

I loved to box. It was a real thrill but I needed some help to increase my courage levels. So I watched other fighters from the sidelines to pick up some tips. They entered the ring filled with confidence and charisma – safe in the knowledge that they'd trained hard and knew their strengths – but when things became difficult, the confidence in their eyes was replaced by fear. In a few moments their hard-earned skills were forgotten, leaving them helpless.

Coaches and other experts told me that successful fighters, like all successful people, don't get scared, they just have 'It'. I really wanted 'It' because I felt fear in all areas of my life. Whether it was public speaking, asking a question in a group, sitting exams, going for a job interview or requesting a bank loan, I would feel those familiar palpitations. Feeling alone in my fear, I questioned my courage levels. What was this mysterious 'It'? How could I get 'It'?

Did luck determine who inherited the wonderful genes of 'It'?

Haunted by these thoughts, I read all I could on the subject of fear. I completed a degree in psychology but still the answers did not come. I began to think that maybe there were certain people who just didn't feel fear, who had this elusive 'It' that the coaches talked about. I decided to find out.

I started interviewing successful boxers and their coaches. They had much to say on the topic of fear, but not that much on the existence of 'It'. They said they did feel fear, but chose to deal with it differently. I soon learned that the way these people handled fear was universal and not limited to boxing. This inspired me to interview other people who had found success in different areas of life, all of whom had hard-earned reputations for courage. I have named these people Fear Professionals.

I was fortunate enough to be able to interview more than a hundred Fear Professionals. Of those interviewed, more than half were police officers and more than a third were athletes and coaches. When I looked more closely, I discovered ten themes the Fear Professionals all shared when managing fear.

It took me a while, but I have finally found the answers to handling fear. Now you too can learn the ten secrets of the Fear Professionals and turn your fear into power.

Note: Police officers and those who have been quoted during counselling have had their names withheld for privacy reasons.

INTRODUCTION

What is fear?

Fear is an emotional response to danger. The danger could be slight, like being laughed at in a crowd, or lethal, like a shark attack. Either way, our body reacts with fear, which triggers a painful response to fight or to flee a threatening situation. Different manifestations of fear include anxiety, stress, worry, phobia, nervousness and panic. Identifying all the different forms of fear is beyond the scope of this book, so when I mention the term 'fear', I'm referring to the distress you experience when you've stepped out of your comfort zone.

Fear has the potential to either give you the power to step out of your comfort zone or make you a prisoner of it. To help explain how fear has both positive and negative potential we can compare it to water: without it we die, too much and we drown. Yet when properly harnessed, fear, like water, is a life-giving tool. When poured into a vase, water takes the shape of it. So too can fear tailor itself to the situation you are in at the time. Fear is directly related to a person's life experiences, which is why people's fears are so individual. Your fingerprints and even your tongue-print are like no one else's. You are unique, a one of a kind. Your fears are unique to you.

★ Fear – the natural protector

To help explain why fear is a natural protector, you will need to know a little bit about your body. Fear helps trigger chemical and physical changes in your body to protect you against danger, commonly known as the 'fight or flight' response. Let's consider the example of stumbling across a snake during a walk. Your fear will trigger the adrenal gland to secrete a hormone into your bloodstream called adrenaline (or epinephrine). Adrenaline helps to produce a series of specific changes in your body, all with the aim of preparing you to be fully alert against danger. Your heart-beat might increase, your blood pressure might rise, your breathing rate might increase – your fear has helped trigger all these reactions in your body for many reasons. Knowing these reasons and that it's normal to experience different responses during fearful situations can empower you.

- **Rapid breathing:** Your lungs are trying to get as much oxygen into your bloodstream as possible. The more oxygen you have in your blood, the easier it is for your brain and major muscles to perform fast physical movements.

- **Increased heart rate:** The oxygenated blood needs to be pumped to your brain and major muscles, and away from areas that don't have an immediate, active role, such as the digestive organs and extremities like skin, hands and feet.

- **Pale face:** As the blood is pumped away from your extremities, the lack of blood causes these areas to become pale and cool to the touch.

- **Need to go to the toilet:** As the blood is directed away from the digestive system and toward the brain, lungs and major skeletal muscles, your digestive system, bowel and bladder are temporarily shut down, which results in non-essential substances being discarded – hence the need to go to the toilet.

- **Dryness of mouth and throat:** Saliva production (which is part of digestion) ceases as the digestive system is temporarily shut down. This also causes a loss of appetite.

- **Sweating and rise in body temperature:** Glucose stored in the liver is released into the bloodstream and converted into energy, ready to be used to meet the threat at hand. This raises the body temperature and causes sweating.

The whole process outlined above occurs unconsciously in 8–10 seconds. So the next time you experience these symptoms before a fearful situation, rest assured that this is perfectly normal. The knowledge that these responses are designed to help you will assist you in managing them. The physical symptoms of fear are making you alert and protecting you against potential harm. This protection makes fear valuable.

Even though it's normal to feel fear when facing a new challenge, fear can be regarded as a problem when it interferes with your:

- everyday living
- achievement of desired goals
- reasonable emotional comfort.

'You're not weak if you feel fear, you're only weak if you choose to run from it.'

WAYNE BENNETT

Remember, when you are able to beat your fear on one particular day, this doesn't mean it won't be back the next. It's like brushing your teeth: just because you brush them once doesn't mean they're protected against decay for the rest of your life. You cannot beat fear but you can use it to your advantage. Fear is power. Make your fear work for you.

CHAPTER 1

We all feel fear

'Fear is a very strong motivating factor; fear of failure is one of the central components of success.'

Alan Jones, media personality and former coach of the Australian Wallabies rugby union team

'To say I'm not afraid to get hurt would be a lie. All boxers are afraid of getting hurt, but I've learned how to control my fear.'

Kostya Tszyu, world boxing champion

Would you like to learn how to let fear help you reach your full potential in life? Whether your goal is to make more money, become more influential, have happier relationships or play better sport, by applying the techniques in this book you will achieve more in your life than you ever thought possible.

We all feel fear. That's the first point to realise. It's those who know how to harness and direct their fear effectively who are able to convert it into a valuable tool. They have a secret advantage over the rest of the population, an advantage we can all access if we know how. This book will teach you the Fear Professionals' secrets of tapping into the power of fear, power that is available to all of us.

I use the term 'Fear Professionals' to refer to people who choose professions or sports that involve the risk of danger and, therefore, high levels of fear. These include shark diving experts, police officers, professional athletes, famous explorers and even a lion tamer.

These Fear Professionals have made careers out of constantly exposing themselves to frightening situations and not only do they admit to feeling fear, but they actually welcome it. The ability to use fear as an asset instead of a weakness makes their courage levels unique, setting them apart as winners. Their insights will help you demystify the often misunderstood emotion of fear.

What is your fear? Is it ending a bad relationship? Being judged for wearing the same old clothes? Dying? Going to the toilet in the dark? Whatever it is, you can apply the simple but effective techniques that Fear Professionals use. Even though most of us don't put ourselves in regular life-threatening situations like Fear Professionals do, the point is that we, like them, feel fear. Our fears, no matter what they happen to be, are very real to us.

Before interviewing the Fear Professionals, I expected that they would see fear as negative. I thought that Fear Professionals were fearless because they were exposed to fear on such a regular basis. Surely they would get used to it, right? WRONG!

MYTH 1

BRAVE PEOPLE DO NOT FEEL FEAR.

Fear Professionals know that just because they are regularly exposed to fear, does not mean they are immune from it. On the contrary, they understand that you can never get rid of fear. What you *can* do is learn to live with it. You can control your fear in one situation or area of your life, yet fear may return in another form or when you're in a different situation.

Many people feel that their fear is biologically caused, not learned. In some cases this is true. But many cling to this belief in all situations and accept that controlling their fear is out of their hands. The truth is that for many of us, we are fearful in particular situations and courageous in others. One of my clients is a perfect example: she is a young mother who is scared of being assertive in social situations, but is quite prepared to go through childbirth for a second child. Her fear to courage ratio changes in different scenarios.

'Fear is relative to you, your situation and what is happening at the time.'
PAUL ISGRO

Fear affects us all at every level of our lives: socially, economically, academically, in business, in family life, at work and at play. It is ever-present from the day we are born until the day we die. The truth is that we never get rid of it. We either learn to live with fear or it rules us. This is an insight Fear Professionals have learned to exploit.

Joe Bugner, former world heavyweight boxing champion, fought Muhammad Ali twice, going the distance on both occasions. He received advice from the great fighter that stayed with him for years. 'Muhammad Ali told me a long time ago that any man who goes into the boxing ring without fear is a fool, for the simple reason that they have no idea or understanding of the sport they are doing. Because, he said, without fear you have no resistance, you don't have the extra perception or the quickness or the sharpness to avoid punishment.'

Mark Taylor, former cricket captain for Australia, agreed. 'There is always a certain amount of fear when you go out there to bat. Especially as an opening batsman, I had the fear of the unknown. I think that it's the way you handle this fear that makes the difference between a good player and a great player. What helped me handle my fear was knowing that, chances were, all the other players on the field would be feeling just as nervous as I was.'

It's refreshing to discover that even our elite sportspeople feel some version of the fear we feel at an everyday level. But it's not just the more glamorous of us who combat fear in the workplace. Police scuba divers have to scour rivers, dams and drains for murder weapons and deceased persons, often without being able to see their hands in front of their faces. Business owners tackle thoughts of bankruptcy and theft. Neville Kennard, a successful Australian businessman, explained, 'Most businesses are influenced if not ruled by fear; that is why we buy insurance.'

A police diver in training. (Photo: Mike Combe, NSW Police Public Affairs)

Fear plays such a large role in our lives that often it affects us in ways we would not realise. Because there's a stigma attached to admitting fear, our unmanaged fears soon flow into other areas and restrict our lives. Consider the following examples:

- Charles talks frequently about getting married and having a family. He has always pictured himself settled and happy but hasn't considered the steps he might need to take to get there. There are women he might be attracted to, but the fear of rejection keeps him from ever going out on a date.

- Priscilla decides to ask her boss for a raise. She prepares mental notes as to why she deserves a better salary and is convincing, in her own mind, before the big day. When the meeting arrives, she becomes terrified by the confrontation; she talks too quickly and forgets half of her argument. Priscilla ends up leaving the interview with her self-esteem shredded and no raise.

- Arnold buys a DVD player but gets home only to realise his wife has received one for her birthday. He no longer needs the one he purchased, and he could use the money for other expenses, but the fear of returning items to the store and risking confrontation seems too great. He keeps the player (and the credit card bill).

The truth of the matter is that it is not fear that lets you down. You let yourself down by not tapping into it. Unfortunately, most people don't want their fear improved, they want it removed. By hating your fear you are allowing it to overwhelm you. When fear overwhelms you, it's nearly impossible to turn the situation around so that you feel in control.

 FEAR FACT

Most people want their fear removed, not improved.

★ 'BUT MOVIE STARS DON'T GET SCARED!' HOW DO WE SEE FEAR?

We are often led to believe that success is based on not feeling fear. When action heroes fight villains on moving trains or romantic leads sweep their co-stars off their feet, we assume they do so without being 'limited' by fear. We usually only hear the confident assertions of tennis players before they take centre court, never their nerves. The underlying message is that if you feel fear then you are weak and inadequate. This is just a façade, though. The Fear Professionals know that claiming to have no fear or wanting to crush, destroy, conquer or get over it are sure recipes for disaster.

Steve Van Zwieten, an expert in security and surveillance, has resolved countless threatening and confrontational situations. He summed it up perfectly: 'In over twenty-two years of working in the security game, I have never worked with anyone I respect who says, "I don't get scared". A person who has no fear in a particular area – maybe. A person who has no fear in all areas – impossible.'

'If you aren't nervous when facing a new challenge then you aren't ready.'

JEFF FENECH

The world of elite athletes is no different. Even though physically they might be more impressive – almost superhuman at times – and their mental grit is not to be sneezed at, our sports heroes have the same emotional and physical triggers as we do. Alan Jones, a veteran of the sports world, coached the Australian Wallabies rugby team in the 1980s and since then has helped countless top athletes succeed. When I asked whether elite athletes feel fear or not, his response was unequivocal: 'Forget all the rhetoric and rubbish you are told. From Ian Thorpe to Patrick Rafter to Kylie Minogue, all great performers experience fear. They are human beings just like you and me. They sleep as you sleep, they wake up as you wake up, and they have moments of self-doubt just as we all do.'

Alan Jones gives pre-game advice to two Wallabies players.
(Photo: Alan Jones)

The Perceived Fear Scale

Fearful	Fearless
Average people	Hollywood action heroes
You and me	Fear Professionals

 ### The Actual Fear Scale

Fearful	Fearless
Average people	Liars
You and me	Fools
Hollywood action heroes	
Fear Professionals	

Often we have the perception that we should not feel fear. Most of us would rather it be surgically removed than recognised. But the truth is that we all feel fear in some area of our lives. The person who doesn't know the meaning of the word 'fear' probably doesn't know the meaning of many other words either.

If it's any consolation, psychologists have found that most emotional mood states such as fear can't be blocked out by sheer willpower. This means it's not a lack of discipline on your part, or a sign of weakness. Any attempts to block out your fear are likely to be unsuccessful and, in the end, these failures may just make you feel worse.

> **'We keep fears to ourselves because of the fear of looking vulnerable. Tough people don't like to admit that they are a sissy or that they cry watching *Lassie*.'**
>
> CRAIG MORDEY

Apart from trying to block out your fear with willpower, one of the worst ways you can mismanage it is by comparing your fears with other people. This will set you up for failure because your fears are based on your own life experiences, just as other people's fears are based on their life experiences. Everyone is different.

What scares one person may not scare another. I learned this from a boxer who didn't want his name mentioned for fear it would tarnish his career (his worst fear). For our purposes, let's call him Bob. When I first saw Bob, he was in the gym, pulverising a heavy punching bag. Covered in tattoos and snarling each time he hit the bag, Bob was a fearsome sight – certainly not someone you would want to meet in a dark alley. After he had finished training I took a deep breath and approached him for an interview on the topic of fear. It was ironic; my heart was racing I was so nervous and I wanted to interview Bob about fear! I was surprised when he agreed to the interview and felt shocked when he shared a very personal fear he had. Bob, the fearless fighter, was terrified about getting married and having to dance the bridal waltz in front of a large crowd. He'd avoided dancing all his life because of his 'two left feet' and worried that once others saw how uncoordinated he was, they'd laugh him off the dance floor. The fact that he was coordinated in the boxing ring hadn't occurred to him. The boxing ring was his comfort zone; the dance floor was not.

The interview ended on a happy note by discussing the possibility of dancing lessons. Bob went away feeling a little more assured and I came away with an important lesson: no matter who you are, once you leave your comfort zone, chances are you will feel fear. This goes for anyone, yourself included. The bottom line is we all feel fear. It is the way you manage your fear that is crucial.

'Everyone's fears are different but we all feel fear. Boxing is a funny sport because boxers all act tough, though get scared if they get a runny nose, a cold or some other health complaint before a fight.'

DR LOU LEWIS

★ MANAGING FEAR – THE TRADITIONAL REMEDY

Shortly you will learn how to correctly handle fear, though it's just as important to know how not to manage it. We've looked at the old school of thought, which sees fear as a figment of the imagination and expects a person to just 'snap out of it'. This 'classic cure' works by implying that fear is not warranted. This idea is most clearly illustrated in the common story of the child who is scared of the water. His parents know how important it is that their son learns to swim so the father resorts to the classic cure for fear and throws the boy in the deep end, saying, 'Face your fear, son, you can beat it!'

This example may seem extreme nowadays. But many of us feel the only way to deal with fear is to face it head on. Such an approach can be potentially disastrous to both your confidence and physical wellbeing. The boy scared of the pool may have learned to swim but at what cost? Would he instead develop an avoidance of swimming or a mistrust of his parents and other authority figures?

It is little wonder that for many people facing fear is an agonising experience. Have you done something new that was absolutely terrifying, only to resolve that you would never allow yourself to be caught like that again? You may have faced your fear, but the 'cure' ended up being far worse than the complaint. Be wary of this supposedly classic cure for fear. As you will learn throughout this book, Fear Professionals do not face a fear just to be rid of it. Instead they choose a specific style to manage it.

★ THE THREE STYLES FOR MANAGING FEAR

How do you respond to fear? There are three basic styles people use to manage fear: Under-reaction, Overreaction, and Harnessing.

Under-reaction sees fear as destructive and tries to make you ignore it altogether. This results in having a false sense of confidence. Overreacting to fear will make you repel fear at all costs in any potentially fearful situation. This stops people from ever stepping out of their comfort zone. Finally, Harnessing, used by Fear Professionals, neither tries to ignore fear nor repel it. Instead, this style acknowledges fear as both normal and as a valuable asset.

Of these three styles, only Harnessing is helpful. This is the one you will be learning to apply to fear in your life. It is worth examining Under-reaction and Overreaction to see why these two are not as effective.

UNDER-REACTION

On the surface, a person using an under-reacting style for managing fear comes across as extremely confident and carefree. But this confidence is usually a thin veneer that is easily broken. The under-reactor sees fear as destructive and tries to ignore it. He is led into a false sense of security by the assumption that if fear and the associated risks it is alerting them to are ignored, then everything will be alright. Favourite under-reacting phrases of reassurance are: Don't worry; What could possibly go wrong?; and There's nothing to be scared of.

OVERREACTION

At one time or another we have probably all overreacted to fear. The overreacting style's main aim is to repel fear and its associated feelings as quickly as possible.

Overreaction often encourages helplessness by blanketing a person with perpetual panic. This might result in the overreactor embarrassing herself by becoming highly emotional, irrational and helpless because only the worst possible situation springs to mind, without any solutions. Favourite overreacting phrases are: It's too risky; I won't be able to handle it; and This is all going to end badly.

HARNESSING

The third style of managing fear, which the Fear Professionals use, is Harnessing. What do I mean by this? Harnessing fear is accepting and respecting it as both normal and as a source of power. The Harnessing style looks to rechannel fear and use it positively. The simplest way of doing this is to actually welcome fear and listen to what it has to say. Favourite Harnessing phrases are: It's okay to be scared; What's my fear telling me?; and Fear is good.

Let's look at some scenarios and the different reactions all three styles would give.

1. You have to sign a legal document in order to buy the house you love but the document is confusing.

    Under-reaction: You don't bother to read the fine print and just sign it. It'll be okay.

    Overreaction: You don't sign it at all because the legal jargon is just too overwhelming.

    Harnessing: You get an expert to read over the fine print on the document before signing it.

2. You have been asked to give a public talk on a subject you're quite familiar with.

   Under-reaction: You don't make the effort to prepare material and instead expect to make it up on the spot, which results in a disorganised and rambling speech.

   Overreaction: During the speech, you freeze due to fear, and forget your words.

   Harnessing: You become invigorated by your fear prior to giving the speech, which inspires you to prepare properly.

3. Your teenage son has not come home and it is past his curfew.

   Under-reaction: You reason that he'll be home in the morning, and go to bed without doing anything.

   Overreaction: You call the police to search for your son only ten minutes past his curfew.

   Harnessing: You determine a reasonable amount of time to wait before contacting the appropriate people.

 FEAR FACT
Under-reaction ignores fear.
Overreaction repels fear.
Harnessing rechannels fear.

Before you label yourself with one of the two negative fear management styles, keep in mind that people are not total overreactors or under-reactors. Instead we often fluctuate between the two, depending on the situation. You may overreact to the fear of flying yet under-react to the fear of being involved in a car accident. Psychologists have found it is nearly impossible to place people in boxes because we often fall between categories. The under-reacting and overreacting styles do not attempt to classify a person's personality. Instead they are concerned with a person's behaviour in reference to the current fearful situation being faced. This is because a person's behaviour can, and often does, change depending on the immediate circumstances.

> ### 'You wouldn't be human if you didn't feel nerves before a competition.'
> TONY MUNDINE SNR

Both Under-reaction and Overreaction attempt to achieve the same impossible task: to beat fear through avoidance. If these two styles are inadequate, what makes the third style, Harnessing fear, so different? It relies on one important component. It is based on the first of the Fear Professionals' ten secrets.

Secret 1
FEAR IS POWER

Fear Professionals have learned to see their fear as a positive force that is designed to help them. Knowing that fear is power makes harnessing this positive energy possible. The key to using the first secret is learning to perceive your fear as an asset – as pure power running through your veins. This is such a crucial point that it cannot be emphasised enough. By completely accepting that fear is power you can tap the phenomenal energy of this secret, harnessing it in the same way as the Fear Professionals do.

Steve Van Zwieten explained the importance of perceiving fear as power: 'When the adrenaline starts flowing, you have to believe that you are primed and ready to go. The minute you start focusing on and hating this feeling caused by fear, it takes away that advantage you have by feeling scared. If you see your nerves as an advantage, then this will give you strength.'

Alan Jones further reinforced this concept: 'It's okay to admit feeling a bit of fear or nerves. And you should admit to nerves. Someone who doesn't admit he or she is nervous before major competition is a shonk. But the key to a winner is they don't allow the nervous energy to limit a performance. Rather, it should invigorate it. Take on a positive "Although I'll be nervous, it will make me stronger and more alert. So when I hit that water, or the gun goes off on the track, or the whistle blows, then I'll just open up."'

★ HARNESSING FEAR'S POWER

People often become confused when I tell them that Fear Professionals see fear as power. This is not surprising, especially if you feel your fear has made you react in ways that were not beneficial. In order to see your fear as power, it's important to be aware you have a choice in the way you perceive it. Either you can see it as a harmful weakness, like the majority of people, or you can see it through the eyes of a Fear Professional – as a positive force there to help you.

> **'Everyone has got fear in them; it all depends what a person does with their fear which makes them a hero or a coward.'**
> TROY WATERS

Fear is designed to protect you in times of immense challenge by giving strength and a heightened state of awareness. This acts as an alarm, passed down from our earliest ancestors, which warns of possible approaching danger. Their fear told them whether to fight or flee when faced with danger. A Fear Professional capitalises on this fear, perceiving it as a protective asset instead of a burden.

Compare fear to a seatbelt. For a small child squirming to escape restriction, a seat belt is a nuisance. But for the elite Formula One driver, the seatbelt provides life-preserving safety and instils confidence and courage. Fear, like the seatbelt, is a necessity for our own safety. But it is how you perceive fear that makes the difference.

The cornerstone of a Fear Professional's courage is acknowledging fear as a positive force. Jim Cassidy, winning jockey of two Melbourne Cups, said, 'The day I stop getting butterflies before a race is the day I know I've lost that fire in the belly to keep me achieving.'

So why do the rest of us have so much difficulty choosing to see fear as power? Researcher on fear, psychologist Dr Stanley Rachman from the University of British Columbia, suggests people are inclined to associate fear with vivid experiences of pain. This association with pain may be physical, such as becoming injured, or the pain may be emotional, like feeling humiliated after making a fool of yourself in public. In both cases, what your fear is trying to do is protect you.

If you're having trouble believing fear is protective, consider a person heavily intoxicated by drugs or alcohol. Like someone inebriated, those who ignore their fear are uninhibited and superhuman, often taking huge risks like driving a car at high speeds, being verbally abusive in public, or swimming in dangerous waters. Surrounding spectators might stand back and laugh at such behaviour, but a person who acts without fear is heading for disaster.

Dick Smith, the entrepreneur and adventurer, described fear as the ultimate protector in life: 'It makes you conservative so I think fear is very important. The fear that something might go wrong or you might get injured or you might fail – that all makes you far more aware and far more careful to make sure that you reduce the risk as much as possible so you are successful.'

Ron Taylor, the shark diving expert, is someone many might regard as more reckless than Dick Smith, but he agreed whole-heartedly: 'If you had no fear you would do stupid things and probably wouldn't survive. Not knowing when to be fearful can lead to accidents. When you come across a situation you don't understand, back off. For example, I am not a snake expert so I treat all snakes as potentially dangerous.'

Society often teaches us to be afraid of fear. We see it as a hin-drance and a sign of weakness instead of a powerful protector. We go to great lengths to avoid fear and bury it wherever possible. But burying your fear does not mean you have escaped it. All you've done is use the quick-fix, temporary bandaid

Ron Taylor freeing a great white shark that had become entangled in the steel cable attached to their diving cage.
(Photo: Ron and Valerie Taylor)

solution, which does not deal with the actual problem your fear is alerting you to.

To embrace your fear and harness its power, you must first uncover how it has been affecting you. It may seem daunting to uncover your fear but keep in mind you now know that fear is power. Your fear is there to help you.

How can you learn to see your fear as power? In answering this question I think back to the motto a front-line police officer shared, 'Fear – embrace it!' How powerful this statement is! Notice the officer didn't say confront fear, but embrace it. To embrace is to clasp to ourselves what we love and cherish. Learning to treat your fear as a powerful ally, to appreciate it, is the most valuable thing you can do.

Imagine you are about to give a speech and your body is reacting uncontrollably to fear. The more you try to hide your fear, the more it shows its power by controlling your body without your consent: it makes you shake, dries your throat, and unleashes sweat across your palms. Instead of over- or under-reacting to fear, try to welcome and embrace it. Thank your fear for making you alert, stronger and more prepared. You would be amazed at how powerful this simple technique of embracing fear is in harnessing its power. The next step in learning how to embrace fear and harness its power comes through honesty.

★ HONESTY'S ROLE IN EMBRACING FEAR

We go to great pains to hide our fear from other people and, in doing so, we also hide our fear from ourselves. I once saw a bumper sticker that read, 'Real men don't ask for directions'. I remember wondering if that meant that real men were lost. It occurred to me that this sticker represents how the majority of people approach their fear – in denial. So many of us refuse to ask ourselves for directions as to the source of our fear. This is either because we under-react or we overreact. Either way, both methods don't deal with the actual problem that your fear is alerting you to.

Layne Beachley, six-time world champion surfer, talks about this problem:

> 'Become aware of what your fear is. Fear possesses people when they are ruled by it, preventing them from growing and experiencing new things. When you ask a lot of people what they are scared of they will say, "I don't know." So I say to these people, "How in the hell are you going to handle your fear if you don't even know what you're afraid of?"
>
> 'Acknowledge your fear and bring it out in the open. Just doing this simple thing will help you to be less afraid of it.'

Standing up to your fear by acknowledging it and bringing it out into the open, as Layne described, is extremely powerful. This display of courage will give you a sense of relief, like a weight being lifted. Why? Because it takes a tremendous amount of effort to keep fear buried. As a result, all of that energy you'd been using to hold down and ignore your fear is suddenly given

Layne Beachley at the 2002 Billabong Pro in Hawaii. (Photo: AAP Image)

back to you as power, for you to use positively. There's a great saying, 'When you spend your life in a cautionary crouch, the greatest relief of all may come from simply standing up.' So stand up on your fear and acknowledge it. All you are doing is uncovering the problem your fear was alerting you to in the first place. You're not creating more.

Embracing fear may be easier said than done; we often opt to avoid honesty. We fall into the trap of taking the so-called 'easy' way out, assuming that if we ignore our fears and refuse to address them, they will somehow go away. The danger of burying fear is it leaves you with feelings of inferiority and often unconsciously prevents you from doing things that have some element of risk-taking. To avoid being honest about your fear by burying it is a great way of nurturing feelings of inadequacy.

'The way to look at fear is to ask yourself, "Why am I scared?"'

RENATO CORNETT

The reason many people bury their fears is to avoid seeming paranoid, irrational, pessimistic or psychologically unwell. Even worse, they may fear bringing something upon themselves by just thinking about them. Parents are often a prime example of this – they have many fears racing around in their heads that they feel they can't disclose. I see this as both a psychologist and a parent, and when I talk with other parents they begin to share the fears they have been suppressing. Fears for their children's safety range from the child accidentally drinking poison or detergents around the house to being bullied at school, to more extreme fears such as their child being kidnapped, sexually abused, or even murdered.

Often parents feel there must be something wrong with them for thinking such morbid and pessimistic thoughts. The interesting part is that no matter how much they try to ignore their fears by burying them or being logical, they cannot seem to rid these fears from their minds. Once they bring their fears out into the open, parents find that they are not alone and feel a tremendous relief. It takes a lot of energy to bury fear, a bit like trying to keep a huge secret. These parents have empowered themselves by simply being honest and learning to accept that they were normal for having fears.

I was taught this most poignantly by Rebecca, a teenager who developed severe abdominal pains that doctors were unable to diagnose. After numerous tests and scans, the doctors decided to perform a small exploratory operation on her, to make a better diagnosis. Rebecca came to me for help with managing her anxiety as she was terrified of having her first operation. It was her parents' idea that she see me. They were concerned that Rebecca had not got over her fear. But, as Rebecca explained, she had every right to feel fear and to explore its basis. 'My parents think by telling me not to worry I suddenly won't. It's not like a switch that I can turn on and off. Besides, I am about to get operated on for the first time so I should be allowed to be scared, shouldn't I?'

★ UNCOVERING YOUR FEAR: HOW DO YOU START?

One big step in harnessing fear is openly admitting to whatever you are scared of. This may be difficult, especially if you have been unconsciously ignoring or running from your worries. For example, if you have been denying your fear, then it's likely that you will find it difficult to uncover what you are actually afraid of. Likewise, if you are constantly experiencing fear in a multitude of different situations, then it's likely you have never stopped to work out the source of your fear. If either of these examples applies to you, then you would benefit from using the Harnessing style to uncover your fear.

The Fear Professionals' Harnessing style relies heavily on acknowledging fear and what is fuelling it. When interviewing the Fear Professionals, I found that it was the way they honestly looked at their worries that helped them quickly and accurately uncover their fear.

Wayne Bennett, former coach of the Australian Rugby League team, spoke about how he helped a player harness his fear:

> 'To help a player learn to recognise their fear, you first let them know it's okay to feel a bit of fear in the first place. Of course footballers all feel fear – even the big guys. It's a fallacy that only the small guys feel fear; even the big guys feel it, sometimes more. Once I have explained that it is okay to feel fear, I then ask the player to address what the problem is. I talk them through it and help bring their fear to the surface. At times this can be difficult because people are scared to admit feeling fear and a lot of footy players see fear as a weakness and won't say anything. Then I point out the fact that they are already out there doing it, which shows they aren't weak.'

Wayne Bennett (centre) with the Australian Rugby League team. (Photo: AAP Image)

Notice Wayne uses a few steps to help a player uncover his fear. First he lets the player know that it is okay to feel fear. Then he gets the player to address the problem (in a football player's case, it may be suffering from nerves during the lead-up to a game). And finally, Wayne will talk through the problem with the player, to expose the fear and then accurately assess what is fuelling it (the player with 'nerves' prior to a game may feel that if he plays badly, he will be kicked off the team).

This is a powerful sequence of steps to expose fear. Most of us do not have a skilled coach like Wayne Bennett to talk us through uncovering our fear, but we can still apply his principles to our own lives. In chapter 5, Sharing Your Fear, you will learn more about the importance of talking about your fear with trusted others.

Based on Wayne's insights, I have devised the Fear Finder, a three-step process to help you uncover and discover your fear. Go through the Fear Finder's steps and write down your fears on paper. It is an eye-opening challenge that is sure to surprise you.

★ USING THE FEAR FINDER

STEP 1: Accept fear as normal.

STEP 2: Identify the problem situation.

STEP 3: Assess your fear in relation to the situation.

Let's go through the Fear Finder, step by step, so you can get the most out of it.

★ STEP 1: ACCEPT FEAR AS NORMAL

Acknowledge that it's normal for you to feel fear; we all feel it. I've repeated this fact because often the biggest hurdle in learning to embrace fear is getting past the false belief that fear is evil and destructive. Remember, it is normal to feel fear. Accepting this fact paves the way for step two.

★ STEP 2: IDENTIFY THE PROBLEM SITUATION

Often the problem situation will be in areas you are reluctant to face, or avoiding altogether. If you can think of a certain situation you consistently avoid, then it is highly likely it will be the basis of your hidden fear. Problem situations you may feel an urge to avoid could be:

- Exercising in public because you are not in shape.

- Attending a mothers' playgroup as a single father.

- Dealing with an authority figure like a teacher or boss.

- Completing an important task because it involves asking for help.

- Committing to a relationship.

- Retraining at a mature age.

Once you have identified your problem situation, then you can move onto the Fear Finder's third step.

★ STEP 3: ASSESS YOUR FEAR IN RELATION TO THE SITUATION

Were you warranted in feeling fear in the situation you felt compelled to avoid? It is perfectly normal to feel nervous when returning items to a shop, dealing with an authority figure or completing a major task. After all, there is the possibility of being embarrassed or humiliated, which we generally try to avoid. Simply knowing that fear is normal in such a situation helps alleviate thoughts that there must be something wrong with you for feeling this way. Taking ownership of your fear as a common human trait is extremely empowering and helps prevent you from identifying yourself as the problem.

★ SEEING IS BELIEVING - WRITE YOUR FEARS DOWN ON PAPER

To increase its effectiveness when using the Fear Finder, write your fears down on paper. We have spent so much of our lives avoiding or ignoring our fear that when we see the source of our fear written on paper we are more willing to acknowledge it.

It may take you more than one attempt at using the Fear Finder to discover the source of your fear. But lowering your subconscious guard so that you can uncover your fear is not easy. This is especially true if you have been spending much of your life keeping your guard up high so as not to get hurt. Be aware that each step you take toward uncovering your fear will bring you closer to discovering what is fuelling it. Remember that your fear is there for a reason, so take your first step toward courage by being honest about it.

FEAR FACT

Fear is good. Knowing why you are feeling it is even better.

★ BENEFITS OF USING FEAR'S POWER

Let's recap on the benefits of choosing to see fear as power. Firstly, it lets you know that it is normal to feel fear because we all feel it. Secondly, you can learn to re-channel fear's power to motivate you to focus fully on the task at hand. Whether it's being scared of performing a task and re-injuring yourself, making new friends, walking through a park where a magpie is known to swoop, going to counselling for the first time or attending a school reunion, your fear is there to help you by increasing confidence, strength and alertness. The moment you can openly and honestly acknowledge your fear and embrace it, you are on your way to taking on fear's power as your own. You become the master and fear becomes your servant.

EXERCISE

Each day do something small that scares you (preferably nothing dangerous). It may be the phone call to a friend you have been putting off, inquiring about further education, asking someone for something or simply exploring a new area. Just do the thing you have been putting off doing because you are afraid of it.

CHAPTER SUMMARY

1. There is no such thing as fearless people in society, because we all feel fear.

2. Fear is a protector designed to increase strength and alertness.

3. Fear Professionals accept and respect their fear, welcoming it as a powerful asset designed to protect them.

4. The Fear Professionals' first secret – *Fear is power*.

5. How to use the Fear Finder to uncover and discover your fear so it can be used to your advantage.

CHAPTER 2

What you CAN control

'All the athletes and celebrities I have met through my travels have admitted to the same thing: you never get over your fear, you just learn to control it.'

Joe Bugner, former world heavyweight boxing champion

'Being in control of a fearful situation is a matter of understanding yourself.'

Ron Taylor, shark diving expert

A close encounter with a great white shark would be, for most of us, a terrifying experience. For Ron Taylor, it's all in a day's work. But it's not without fear, as he recounts here.

> 'When I was filming *Jaws* I was in a situation where I was in a cage underneath the water and there were baits in the water to attract sharks. There was a large great white shark circling the cage. I had a movie camera to film the shark but the bars in the cage were getting in the way of filming, so I was half hanging out the top of the cage to get a clear shot of the great white. The shark was swimming around me, and it wasn't really that interested. Then suddenly it saw me and came straight for me. I thought, "This is great. It's coming straight for me so I'll just keep filming and then I'll drop down in the cage at the last moment." But when I started to go down, my scuba tank on my back went down the outside of the cage and my feet went down the inside. I was stuck and couldn't get down into the cage. I suddenly realised that this was not good. I only had to come up a short distance to untangle my tank from the cage, but I didn't have time as I would have been even more exposed. So all I did was push my camera toward the oncoming shark's face. Interestingly, the shark kept coming for me and it pushed the camera, myself and the cage to the side, and kept going. My heart was beating a little bit fast then! However, I was able to not panic and remain calm, which probably saved my life.'

As in Ron's example, being able to remain calm and not panic in a fearful situation is an impressive skill to have. It doesn't come naturally to us all though.

- Do you blush when having to explain yourself to others?

- Is sounding confident over the phone difficult for you?

- Would you like to be able to remain calm when facing uncertain situations?

Having a better understanding of what makes fear tick and how to control it will give you an invaluable tool to remain calm in the most stressful situations.

What is it that allows Fear Professionals like Ron Taylor to remain calm and keep their cool in threatening situations? In one word – control. In this chapter you will learn how Fear Professionals are able to take control of situations that, to you and me, would appear hopeless. You'll discover what a special-forces police officer focuses on to control a rioting crowd. Find out how Fear Professionals treat the concept of luck in relation to facing a fearful situation. Uncover what a Fear Behaviour Pattern is and how to observe and then change its insidious influence on your life. And finally, learn a technique that helps you increase confidence to face your fear, all done in the safety of a practice situation.

Fear Professionals are constantly dealing with the task of remaining calm in scary situations. If Fear Professionals are not in control, then it could cost them their lives. What they aim to control is usually very different to what we might expect. They do not try to control the things around them such as people, animals and objects. Fear Professionals put their full effort into controlling their own reaction to a situation. In Ron's case, he couldn't control the shark but he could control his own actions.

You may have thought that the aim of Fear Professionals must be to control the situation, which would mean being in control of the people and things around them, otherwise they would not be calm, right? WRONG!

MYTH 2

SUCCESSFUL PEOPLE CAN CONTROL THEIR ENVIRONMENT.

Fear Professionals do not think that they must control things that are uncontrollable. This second myth highlights a common misconception that to be in control of ourselves and remain calm, we must first control everything around us. The problem with this is that we have no control whatsoever over what is around us. It makes no difference whether it is taking out a loan and sweating on interest rates, driving a car in peak hour traffic or wanting to beat your competitors. You do not have full control over these situations.

Layne Beachley takes this mindset into surfing competitions. 'If you can control yourself on the inside and remain calm and focused, you have a greater chance of controlling what is happening outside.'

One of the police officers interviewed felt similarly, giving much-needed insight into the reality of charged situations. 'In a confrontation, both the officer and the offender are usually just as scared as each other. Therefore if you can control your reaction by managing your fear, you suddenly have an advantage.'

Fear Professionals, whether working with people or animals, all focus on controlling their own reactions. Even when it seems that they have somehow bewitched the animals, the Fear Professionals have actually worked on themselves first and foremost. Tony Gasser Jnr was the world's youngest lion tamer when he began at the age of fifteen. He would step into the cage, surrounded by lions, and still believes that being able to train them is based on one simple principle: 'Call it the bluff, but I knew if I could control myself, then I could control the lions.' If the lions sensed he was not in control of his own reactions, then he would inadvertently be showing that he was also not in control of the situation. This spells trouble if you are surrounded by lions.

All Fear Professionals said that they did not have control over the things and people around them. But it was difficult to resist the urge to say, 'No, that can't be.' I felt that this might succeed for them, but if I were to apply this idea to my life, I would be lowering my guard and making myself vulnerable. By really listening to these Fear Professionals and applying this concept in my own life, I found that it works.

Let's use parents as an example again. Many believe that they should have control over their child from birth. If the parents are not able to control their child during the different maturing stages, then they deem themselves failures. But how much control does a parent really have over their child? Take a look and see:

- The baby cries when it is hungry, not when the parent thinks it should be fed.

- The child sleeps for as long as it wants to, not necessarily at the same time as the parent.

- The child learns to crawl and walk when the *child* is ready, not when the parents want it to.

- The child decides who their friends will be, much to the horror of some parents.

Temper tantrums, messy bedrooms, wagging school, loud music, drugs and sexual activity – from the very beginning, parents do not have full control over their children. This may seem bleak, perhaps even providing a scapegoat for bad parenting? On the contrary, the only thing you have full control over in this world is YOU. Nothing more and nothing less. Now here is the good news: by being able to control your own response to a situation, you are far more likely to influence another person's behaviour. There is a saying I like, 'Life is 10 per cent what happens to me and 90 per cent how I react to it.' It's therefore the way the parent responds to the child that will have the most impact, and the only thing a parent has full control over anyway.

Parenting is one of many areas over which people do not have full control. We can't control the weather, the stockmarket, the actions of other drivers – all we have full control over in this world is our response to situations, a secret that Fear Professionals have learned to harness. They know that the degree to which they control their actions will determine how effectively they respond. Therefore when a Fear Professional is feeling fear, they focus on what can be controlled – their response to the situation not the situation itself.

Many people fail to accept what they have full control over. This leads to giving up control of the most powerful possession a person has.

★ WHY DO WE GIVE UP CONTROL?

What causes you to voluntarily give up the greatest power you possess – control over your reactions to a situation? The answer is trying to control everything except your own reactions. Quite often we have unreal expectations of what we must achieve or, more importantly, what we have to control. Then, when we cannot control these external factors like people, animals, objects and the environment, we give up.

'Once you lose control, you lose.'
DAVID GRAINGER

As children, many of us were taught to give up our sense of control. I was at a friend's house and his young daughter fell off a chair and began to cry. In an attempt to calm her down, he pretended to blame the chair by saying, 'Naughty chair'. His daughter stopped crying but, by blaming the chair, she is learning not to take responsibility for her own actions and, ultimately, that she is not in control of herself. Once we feel we no longer have control over a situation or even ourselves we resort to the age-old belief in 'luck' as a solution to the problem.

★ LUCK vs CONTROL

There is an old saying, 'Success is a matter of luck, ask any failure.' Psychologists claim that one way people are able to gain a sense of control when dealing with fearful situations is by relying on luck.

A young pianist named Mark came to see me because his performances were not consistent. He would often fall victim to nerves just before a competition and, as a result, perform badly. When discussing this, Mark said that each time he performed badly, his family and friends would try to offer encouragement by saying things such as, 'You were unlucky this time but next time you'll have more luck.' It became clear that Mark had developed a belief that his performances, whether successful or not, were based on luck and totally out of his hands. On the days he performed well, Mark attributed his success to luck. He didn't acknowledge that he was controlling his reactions to 'stage nerves' with slow breathing and focusing on the music to remove distractions. On the days he succumbed to nerves and didn't perform so well, Mark felt he was unlucky for feeling fear. This might make us feel better in the short-term, but it isn't a recipe for success, though it's one many of us use when trying to handle our fear.

Fear Professionals who are consistently confident in fearful situations are not 'somehow lucky that they do not feel fear'; we all feel fear. Fear Professionals never rely on luck but instead depend upon control. Why? Because Fear Professionals have learned that, in their line of work, if they were to solely rely on the intangible and unpredictable concept of luck, the chances of failing would be high.

Now there are situations in life that are fortunate, giving credence to the idea of 'luck'. I'm not here to argue that luck does not exist. Whether it be winning a raffle or finding the ideal parking spot while shopping, we have all been lucky at some point in our lives. What Fear Professionals have learned is not to put their full faith in luck, because luck is unpredictable and something over which we have no control. If luck does come your way, make the most of it. But to rely solely on luck when dealing with fear can be lethal.

FEAR FACT
Luck is a lottery. Self-control is a certainty.

If you would like to learn how to rely on control instead of luck, the key is to change the way you respond to situations. To do this you need to know how to take control of yourself.

This leads us to the Fear Professionals second secret.

Secret 2
CONTROL YOURSELF TO CONTROL YOUR SITUATION

Fear Professionals know the only thing they can fully control at any given time is themselves. This is because there will always be someone or something that can beat them, no matter how skilled they are, and the same applies to you. They know that controlling their own reaction to a situation means having a much greater chance of influencing the direction the situation takes. Below are two stories which show Fear Professionals controlling their responses to control the situation.

A police officer who worked in a riot squad told me how controlling his own reactions to fear was a powerful weapon when trying to control an aggressive crowd.

'We'd be dressed in full riot gear, and a vehicle would drop our team off at the danger spot. We'd get out of the vehicle and, as a team, simply jog into position and stand in perfect formation with emotionless faces in front of the approaching rioters. When the rioters would see us, they'd get angry and run at us, screaming and throwing bricks and bottles. We'd stand behind our shields, which would protect us from the full force of the projectiles. We were trained not to get angry, sad, scared or even agitated but simply stand emotionless. You could see it create an uncertainty in their minds. So then the rioters would hurl more personal insults and broken bricks and bottles at us. We'd stand behind our shields, deflecting the projectiles, but still show no emotional reaction.

'It's fascinating to witness the sudden shift in a person's mindset from extremely cocky and aggressive to looks of bewilderment and uncertainty, to finally pure terror. "How can these cops be so controlled and robotic, not showing any form of emotion? We're trying to kill them and they're just standing there. If I were them, there's no way I'd stand there and risk my life. These cops must be crazy."

'Once we knew we had the psychological advantage,

then, on command, we would all run in formation at the rioting crowd. This results in the terrified crowd fleeing in all directions. The whole time we would be concentrating on controlling our own reactions instead of controlling the crowd. We knew if we could control the way we reacted to the crowd, we would be far more likely to be able to control the crowd.'

Now these riot squad officers, when placed in terrifying situations, are vastly outnumbered by hostile crowds. The officer I interviewed openly admitted that he felt fear and rightly so. 'Of course we feel fear. When the angry crowd rushes you, every instinct in your body tells you to run.' So why don't these officers run? Along with their specialised training, they firstly acknowledge to themselves that they are feeling a very normal emotion – fear. Then they concentrate on controlling their reactions to the hostile crowd. The important point to note is that the officers accepted that they could not control the crowd's reactions. Instead, all they could control was their own reaction. By accepting that they only have control over themselves and not the situation, the officers influenced the crowd's behaviour and ultimately took control of the situation.

Front-line police officers, without riot gear, are called in to control rioting protestors. (Photo: Mike Combe, NSW Police Public Affairs)

Valerie Taylor, the shark diving expert, has a similar story of controlled reactions, this time about a non-Fear Professional in a Fear Professional's environment.

'I was working with a Hollywood actor who wanted to feed a moray eel and I instructed him how to do it. I told him, "If things go wrong and it bites, whatever you do don't pull away. It might drag your hand into its hole. Let it go because it will let go and then you will get your hand back in one piece." Would you believe the eel bit his hand? The huge eel had got his hand in its mouth and started to drag him away. The actor, remembering what he had been taught, let the eel drag him toward its hole. The eel, realising that something wasn't right, let go of the actor's hand and all he had was three puncture marks. However, if the actor had tried to pull away, he would have had a lacerated hand. There is a way to do these things but the average person can't do it. That is because the natural reaction is to pull away and not wait for the animal to let go.'

The actor in this scenario had no control over what the eel did, but by controlling his own reactions, he influenced the eel's behaviour.

Large sea eels, when feeding, have the ability to sever a person's hand.

In these examples, the situations were successfully handled because the Fear Professionals took control of their own reaction to the situation. This may sound too simple to be true. But keeping things simple when using any technique to control your fear is essential. If it is not simple, chances are it will be forgotten when the emotions start to flow. What makes the concept of controlling yourself to control your situation so effective?

★ CONTROL YOURSELF TO CONTROL YOUR SITUATION — HOW DOES IT WORK?

Aiming to control yourself to control your situation is powerful because it encourages you to focus on your performance instead of the outcome of a situation. As we've said before, all you have full control over while facing a fearful situation is your own reaction or performance.

Have you ever tripped over in public, sprawling across the ground in front of a large crowd of people? An embarrassing experience. One reason tripping over in public is so humiliating is because you are displaying publicly that you have no control over yourself. And control over our actions is paramount. So why is it that when it comes to an important situation where we want to succeed — making business deals, confronting an annoying neighbour, asking someone out on a first date — we suddenly forget about controlling ourselves and instead focus on controlling the outcome of the situation?

When you're busy trying to control other people or things in a situation, you lose track of controlling your own reaction. Take the example of making a complaint to a boss. Ted feels that his manager, Ms McMahon, has been overloading him with other colleagues' work. He has mentioned it in passing once before but Ms McMahon managed to sidestep the issue by implying that

Ted was not dedicated enough. He decides to address it formally and tells himself, 'This time I won't let her bully me into dismissing the problem. I'll stand my ground.' It is not far into the discussion that Ms McMahon begins to employ guilt tactics and Ted quickly realises he is not going to change her mind. Instead of standing his ground, he feels himself wanting to backtrack out of the conversation. The end result? Ted's strong intentions fade and he is manipulated into agreeing to dismiss the whole thing.

What happened in this scenario? Basically Ted tried to control Ms McMahon's reaction and lost sight of controlling his own. When he tried to control the outcome, or in this case Ms McMahon's opinion, and it didn't work, Ted felt hopeless and gave up. What should he have done? Consider the police officer's earlier example – he did not try to control the rioting crowd but his reaction to it. The actor also did not try to control the eel that bit his hand. Ted needs to focus on controlling his own reaction to the situation instead of controlling his manager's.

With that in mind, let's revisit Ted's scenario and put yourself in his shoes for a moment. This time try to focus on your own response. You may achieve this by:

- monitoring your posture – walk, stand and sit tall, which creates confidence and prevents body language that reinforces defensiveness or submissiveness

- maintaining eye contact

- using deep, slow breathing

- speaking slowly and clearly

- acknowledging your uncomfortable feelings as normal.

Focusing on controlling your own reaction will greatly enhance your ability to maintain a visibly calm composure, which allows you to get your point across more effectively. You will know if this self-control has impacted on your boss if she suddenly resorts to another approach. (NOTE: How to control yourself when dealing with bullies will be discussed in more detail in chapter 6, End a Bully's Mind Games.)

You now know that all you can control is your own response to a situation. But what if you react negatively to stressful situations without realising it or being able to control it at the time? You may turn bright red when asked a question, say 'yes' to something that you don't want to do, or panic when faced with an uncomfortable situation. Is there anything you can do to take control over yourself and become calmer in stressful situations? The good news is that there is. The key is to develop an awareness of your Fear Behaviour Patterns.

★ WHAT IS MY FEAR BEHAVIOUR PATTERN?

A Fear Behaviour Pattern is a pattern of behaviour that causes you to react automatically when you're out of your comfort zone. We all have Fear Behaviour Patterns, some good and some not so good. Certain Fear Behaviour Patterns are necessary for protection and survival, such as running from a snake or screaming when in danger. But some Fear Behaviour Patterns that have the intention of protecting are extremely unhelpful and misguide us to react automatically in situations that are not life-threatening. For example, your Fear Behaviour Pattern may influence you to be submissive when you have to deal with a verbally aggressive person, just to keep the peace. You may be avoiding confrontation, which the body sees as the initial threat, but being submissive may not help you in the long run.

Here are some unhelpful Fear Behaviour Patterns that you may recognise:

1. Peter wants to ask his friend Rosie to return the money he lent her, but because he will not risk possible confrontation, he says nothing and hopes she remembers to pay him back. (Submission)

2. Claire asks for information at a service desk and holds up a line of impatient customers. She begins to feel uncomfortable that she is upsetting the other customers so she ends up telling the assistant not to worry about her request. (Panic)

3. Mary's teacher asks for anyone who knows the solution to a maths equation to write it on the blackboard. Mary knows the answer but says nothing for fear of miscalculating the answer in front of the class. (Avoidance)

Fear Behaviour Patterns are often so powerful that they can occur without your realising. Your autopilot kicks in and you have to stand back as Fear Behaviour Patterns control your actions. Even when your behaviour opposes your own beliefs, like agreeing with others just to keep the peace, your Fear Behaviour Pattern tries to prevent you from getting hurt. Fear Behaviour Patterns are committed to preventing you from stepping out of your comfort zone, especially when new challenges are involved. These patterns do more harm than good – not only do they mis-interpret situations as being physically threatening and try to protect you from them through avoidance, but they also ignore the injuries to your self-esteem. Keep in mind that fear is power only when you are its master. When fear is the master, as is the case with an unhelpful Fear Behaviour Pattern, you become its slave.

FEAR FACT

It's good to feel fear. The key is to be in control of your fear instead of fear controlling you.

Fear Behaviour Patterns can become ingrained. The bad news is that if you keep doing what you always do, you will keep getting what you always get, and nothing will change. Your unhelpful Fear Behaviour Patterns will continue to embarrass and control your life. But the good news is that Fear Behaviour Patterns can be modified. You can learn to take control of them to get the results you want in life.

★ TAKING CONTROL OF YOUR FEAR BEHAVIOUR PATTERNS

How can you take control of your Fear Behaviour Patterns so you can react confidently in stressful situations? First and foremost, you need to become aware of the unhelpful reactions your Fear Behaviour Patterns are causing. This means making a conscious effort to be more aware of your behaviour when you're out of your comfort zone. You have already used the Fear Finder (as outlined in chapter 1) to uncover your fear and bring it out into the open. So you can now step into the next phase of awareness and learn how your Fear Behaviour Pattern encourages you to react.

Think back to a situation where you reacted in a way you didn't like. It may have been a situation such as:

- avoiding eye contact with a person you've just been introduced to
- apologising when things were not your fault
- rebuffing a genuine compliment from someone
- not being able to speak your mind during a meeting
- wanting to say no but feeling unable to.

Knowing what your unhelpful Fear Behaviour Patterns are and the situations that spark them is vital in taking control over yourself. Once you feel you have identified your unhelpful Fear

Behaviour Pattern, the next step is to ask yourself the question, 'Do I want to change the outcome my Fear Behaviour Pattern gives me?'

If your answer is no, and you want to deal with your Fear Behaviour Pattern at another time, then that is fine. The important thing to do is to maintain an awareness of your Fear Behaviour Pattern's existence, which will make dealing with it at a later date much easier.

If your answer is yes and you would like to change the outcome your Fear Behaviour Pattern triggers, then you have the key ingredient to taking control of yourself. Even though having an awareness of your unhelpful Fear Behaviour Pattern is important, it is equally important to have a strong desire to change the unhelpful pattern. It is this willingness to modify an unhelpful pattern that makes Fear Professionals elite in their work. Developing a willingness to change your unhelpful Fear Behaviour Pattern is a highly effective way of increasing your confidence.

Now you are aware of what an unhelpful Fear Behaviour Pattern is. The fact that you are still reading this chapter suggests you have a willingness to alter yours. Congratulations! You are on your way to taking control of old Fear Behaviour Patterns, changing them to do as you wish. To succeed, you will need to start Fear Training.

> **'Fear is energy and it has to be channelled the right way or the athletes will suffer. One way is encouraging them to be productive with their time; understand the benefits of keeping busy.'**
> MICHAEL BROADBRIDGE

★ FEAR TRAINING

Wayne Bennett has said, 'Training is where you sort out all the problems like fear in preparation for the real thing.' This applies to most areas and fear is no different: Fear Training will alter your unhelpful Fear Behaviour Pattern.

Fear Training will increase your self-confidence to face situations without having to actually experience them. It achieves this by revealing how a comfort zone maintains its subtle control over you.

Taking that first step out of a comfort zone requires self-confidence. The biggest obstacle to gaining this self-confidence you will face is the comfort zone itself. That is right, your comfort zone will actually try to stop you from stepping out of it. This is because comfort zones, even if unhelpful, offer protection. Your comfort zone might be avoiding someone you have disagreed with, not going to the movies by yourself, or staying quiet about being harassed at work. The safe side to all these scenarios is that you cannot get hurt or rejected if you do nothing and stay within your comfort zone. The downside is that a comfort zone has a similar effect to a goldfish bowl. A goldfish will only grow as big as the bowl you place it in. The moment you modify your unhelpful Fear Behaviour Pattern and step out of your fishbowl, namely your comfort zone, your chance of growing increases. Why live in a fishbowl when there is a whole ocean out there to be explored? Layne Beachley, who ventures into the ocean each day, knows the pull of the comfort zone. 'You always have to know what your comfort zone is and then be prepared to step out of it, even if it's the smallest of steps.'

'If you step out of a comfort zone, especially when it's a challenge you have never faced before, then of course you are going to get scared. It's good to feel nervous.'

BILL YEARNAN

At this point in time you may feel worried that stepping out of your comfort zone is too daunting. But Fear Training is clever as it gets past your Fear Behaviour Pattern's guard by altering a much smaller pattern of behaviour that is unrelated to your fear. This way you will develop confidence to eventually alter much larger Fear Behaviour Patterns. Kostya Tszyu, the world champion boxer, explained this concept in his interview:

Kostya Tszyu celebrates his victory over Zab Judah in 2001. (Photo: AAP Image)

'Start doing things you don't like to do. Say you don't like getting up at 5 am to exercise, then get up at that time for a week. Or if you have to do homework at 6 pm but there is a movie on, then force yourself to do the homework instead. Train yourself to do the things you don't like to do in everyday life. Make yourself do it and it will become a habit for you to change bigger things in your life that scare you. This will teach you to be brave in other areas of your life.'

To step out of your comfort zone, it's vital that you aim to accomplish something small, something you can realistically achieve. If, for example, you're terrified of doing reverse parks, attempting one during peak hour is unrealistic and asking for trouble. Instead, practise in an empty car park or paddock where you will not be pressured by other drivers.

Gaining control of your Fear Behaviour Pattern through this type of preparation is a secret Fear Professionals have learned to utilise. How then do you apply Fear Training, as displayed in Kostya's example, to unhelpful Fear Behaviour Patterns in your life?

Start by selecting a smaller unhelpful behaviour pattern. Choose a task in your life that you know you should do, or would like to do, but keep putting off. Remember this task has to be relatively easy to achieve and, once again, preferably un-related to your fear. Here is a short list of ideas:

- Start saying hello to a neighbour or person at work you would not normally say hi to.

- Do the washing up straight after dinner if you usually put it off.

- Wear something different from what you normally wear.

- Try playing a new sport.

- Take up a gourmet cooking class.
- Get yourself a new hairstyle.
- Change what you eat for breakfast for a week.

By using physical action to change the smaller behaviour patterns in your life, you are stepping out of your comfort zone. When you step out of your comfort zone, you are altering patterns of behaviour and in turn gaining control over yourself. As soon as you can reclaim control over yourself in one area of your life, this confidence can be channelled into other areas too. With your newly acquired confidence, you are arming yourself to eventually reshape the much stronger Fear Behaviour Pattern that has been holding you back.

> **'Preparation is crucial. If you feel you have done everything you could to prepare yourself for facing your challenge, then this builds confidence.'**
>
> PAUL BRIGGS

Be aware when you start feeling guilty, scared or just uneasy about stepping out of your comfort zone. This is perfectly normal. It is just your old unhelpful Fear Behaviour Pattern trying to prevent you from changing. Resist it. Stay focused. It is normal for your unhelpful pattern to cry out louder as its authority is stripped away. And that's exactly what you are doing – reclaiming control over yourself. To achieve the best results from Fear Training, there are three important points to keep in mind:

1. Be realistic
Whatever your Fear Behaviour Pattern is, be prepared for

gradual change. Learning to gain control over yourself usually occurs in steps. As Alan Jones said, 'Success is incremental. It doesn't come in an avalanche. You know you are not going to move rocks, you are going to move small stones. And hopefully, if you move enough small stones or if you make enough ripples, you will create a tide. But it only starts with a ripple, the tide comes later.'

If you expect instant results, you set yourself up for disappointment and failure. Be kind to yourself. Be realistic and keep the steps small as you move out of your comfort zone. The key to successfully modifying a Fear Behaviour Pattern is taking small continuous steps, which Gaby Kennard, who flew solo around the world, explained, 'I believe that if I approach a fear slowly and carefully, and go a little bit further each day, I will get there.' Going a little further out of your comfort zone each day will bring you closer to reclaiming control over yourself and ultimately to harnessing your fear.

Remember, when taking steps out of a comfort zone it is perfectly normal to feel a little scared and uncomfortable. This shows you are changing.

2. Write down your successes

Modifying a Fear Behaviour Pattern is usually incremental so it's important to record your successes when they occur, no matter how small they seem. Write your victories down in a journal. If during the week you were able to:

- Say hello to one new person at work, write it down.

- Get up early and go for a walk, write it down.

- Have a healthy breakfast, write it down.

These are all victories – writing them down will empower you and increase your confidence because you can reflect on them. This is particularly helpful if you are feeling disheartened about an upcoming challenge. Rereading your successes stops you from thinking that you're failing and motivates you to take bigger steps.

3. Reward courageous behaviour

The third and final point is to reward yourself when you do take steps out of your comfort zone, no matter how small. B. F. Skinner, a psychologist who devoted his life to understanding how people are motivated into action, emphasised the importance of rewards to encourage particular behaviour. After all, our old unhelpful behaviour patterns reward us. Merely having the feelings of fear stopped temporarily by avoidance is a reward in itself. The only problem is that it is a reward that is short-lived and continues to take away our control.

'Dedication ultimately proves better than ability.'

RAY WHEATLEY

It is vital that your new pattern of behaviour also rewards you. At first there may not be any noticeable benefit from your altered pattern, so it's important to reward yourself. When you make progress with your new behaviour pattern, no matter how small, reward yourself with something you like. Whether it's treating yourself to a slice of cake or seeing a movie, rewarding yourself will help reinforce your new behaviour pattern.

 FEAR FACT

Rewarded behaviour gets repeated.

To attain the best results from this chapter, *do* as the old Chinese proverb states:

When you hear something, you will forget it.

When you see something, you will remember it.

But only when you do something, will you understand it.

Therefore let your learning lead to action and *go* step out of your comfort zone.

EXERCISE

Get to know your unhelpful Fear Behaviour Pattern by choosing a small task in your life that you keep putting off. Make sure this task is relatively quick and easy to achieve, but offer a reward for its completion. In both the lead-up to, and performance of, the task notice what your unhelpful Fear Behaviour Pattern wants you to do and then challenge it by doing the opposite. From here you can progress to slightly bigger tasks, all the while modifying your unhelpful Fear Behaviour Pattern.

CHAPTER SUMMARY

1. You do not have full control over other people or situations; you only have full control over yourself.

2. Fear Professionals rely on control instead of luck, which allows them to consistently step out of their comfort zones with successful results.

3. The Fear Professionals' second secret – *Control yourself to control your situation.*

4. Unhelpful Fear Behaviour Patterns cause you to react automatically to fear but, when re-shaped, are the gateway to increasing your confidence.

5. Fear Training is about stepping out of smaller comfort zones to give you the confidence to step out of larger ones.

CHAPTER 3

Consider the worst

'My job as a batsman was to make sure that I won more times than I lost.'

Mark Taylor, former Australian Cricket Captain

'My attitude has always been that anything I do, I make sure it has less risk than driving a car around Sydney.'

Dick Smith, explorer and entrepreneur

Thinking about the worst can actually increase your confidence, but it's often considered destructive or self-defeating. Dick Smith tells of a close friend who resisted considering the worst, which resulted in tragedy:

> 'To reduce the risk as much as possible takes a tremendous amount of organisational management. I was once in Antarctica with a flying friend of mine, Giles Kershaw, one of the most experienced Antarctic pilots in the world, and he said to me, "Dick, you obviously don't enjoy adventure."
>
> 'I said, "Why?"
>
> 'And he said, "Because you are always discussing all the things that could go wrong."
>
> 'I said, "That's right, that's how I work. I discuss everything that could go wrong and then I work out ways of reducing the chance of that happening."
>
> 'He said, "Oh, I never do that. I presume that it's not going to go wrong."
>
> 'Well, unfortunately a year later he died in an air-crash in Antarctica. I always presume everything will go wrong and then I work out ways of reducing that happening. Some people presume everything will go right and then, of course, they don't have the chance of reducing the risk because they already think that there *is* no risk.'

This tragic account illustrates how people often choose to ignore risks associated with a threatening situation, concentrating solely on the positives. Preparing for the worst-case scenario when stepping out of your comfort zone is often discouraged for fear that just thinking about it may somehow cause the worst to happen. For many people the 'It won't happen to me' outlook leads to the belief that the world is a safe place and that, even though bad things happen, somehow they will not happen to them. Psychologists call this the 'illusion of invulnerability'. Examples of this include:

- not replacing batteries in a smoke detector
- propping open a pool-fence gate 'just for a few minutes'
- ignoring 'read before use' directions on a new appliance
- leaving a child in the car while ducking out to the ATM
- not wearing a seatbelt on a short trip.

Unfortunately it is often after a person experiences a major traumatic event that they discard their 'It won't happen to me' blinkers and start considering the worst.

In this chapter you're going to learn how using your naturally occurring pessimism can increase your confidence and reduce the likelihood of the worst happening. To achieve this you will be introduced to the Fear Professionals' main tool of the trade, Positive Pessimism. You will discover why a Fear Professional will not confront a fear simply to be rid of it (shattering the notion that you should confront all fears). And the Fear Professionals reveal the two simple questions they ask themselves to determine whether to face a fearful situation.

How can 'focusing on the worst' help a Fear Professional? After all, Fear Professionals have 100 per cent confidence that they will succeed, never letting a pessimistic thought enter their mind. Otherwise a Fear Professional wouldn't face the fearful situation, right? WRONG!

MYTH 3

IT'S BEST NOT TO THINK ABOUT THE WORST.

When deciding whether to face a fearful situation, Fear Professionals not only accept having thoughts about the worst, but they actually welcome them. Once a Fear Professional has assessed the risks and decided to face a situation, they are subconsciously aware of failure and defeat. This goes against the common belief that to be successful, you must not consider the worst under any circumstances – that you should instead reassure yourself that your fears are exaggerated and that all will go well. But psychologists have found that people naturally justify their actions by twisting the truth to avoid pain. So when it comes to assessing the worst, often we feel a real need to play down the risks and under-react to them. For example, serious car accidents are becoming more frequent but we continue to take unnecessary risks, thinking it won't happen to us.

'A lot of people get injured because they don't know their limitations.'

ROY ALEXANDER

Fear Professionals know that if they consider the worst, they can prepare for the worst. When approaching a situation where the risks are high, Fear Professionals constantly tell themselves that they are not exempt from the worst happening. Doing so keeps them alert and able to react quickly. If you try to handle potential risks by choosing to ignore them, you're at greater risk of being hurt.

It's vital that you use the Fear Professionals' tactic of acknowledging risks when you step out of your comfort zone. When done the right way, acknowledging these risks increases your confidence.

Gaby Kennard explained her reasons for assessing the risks:

'Being optimistic and ignoring the negatives is often what prevents you from handling fear. You need to look at the worst and say, "Well, it's not that bad, I can handle that, and if it happens, so be it." Then, if the worst *does* happen, you're not going to go into a total panic, because you've prepared yourself in your mind by first looking at the worst situation.'

Ron Taylor also admits that when swimming with sharks he always prepares for the worst:

Ron and Valerie Taylor making history by being the first people to both tag a great white shark and take its temperature. The shark's body temperature was 22½ degrees and the water was 18 degrees, which shocked the scientific world by proving that great whites were warm blooded. (Photo: Ron and Valerie Taylor)

'You have to be aware of the negatives. It is of vital importance knowing what could go wrong. Otherwise you would not survive. I am always expecting a problem and try to anticipate it before it happens.

'When diving with sharks I am aware of the risks and, therefore, the risks are reduced dramatically. But the unexpected can still happen. In potentially dangerous situations it's very important to be able to anticipate a potential problem so as to avoid it. Anticipation is very, very important. You look at the situation and, from your experience, you size up the risks and behave accordingly.'

But why should you think about the worst if you're not exposed to the same sorts of risks as the Fear Professionals? Here are some everyday examples of worst-case scenarios that can be prevented if they are not ignored initially:

- Finding you are bound to an unsuitable agreement because you didn't read the fine print before signing.

- Having your car engine blow up because you put off checking the oil or water.

- Discovering that the mole on your arm is malignant, but could have been treated if checked sooner.

These worst-case scenarios can be avoided if they are addressed properly in the early stages. Putting your head in the sand and hoping that, by ignoring risks, they will not happen neglects one fundamental rule: Risks can never be eliminated completely. How often have you ignored risks? We do it all the time – overtaking a slow driver and nearly colliding with oncoming traffic; not backing up your computer only to lose work due to a malfunction; using a power tool without safety glasses and getting something in your eye.

'Of course I get scared, especially when you think that in a fight, one punch can change your whole life forever. Thinking this helps me be ready at all times.'

KOSTYA TSZYU

Risks cannot be eliminated completely. They are a part of life. Yet the way Fear Professionals mentally prepare for these risks seems unconventional. When facing new risks, they tell themselves that they only have an average chance of success. This hardly seems logical as it comes across more like something a defeatist would do rather than someone who has immense courage. The reason why Fear Professionals tell themselves this is that it makes them far more alert to the ever-present possibility of falling victim to risks.

 FEAR FACT

Fear Professionals tell themselves that they only have an average chance of success when facing new challenges.

This advice could easily be dismissed as pessimistic. It would seem better to focus just on your positives and expect a successful outcome. Make no mistake, focusing on the positives and being confident are beneficial to your wellbeing. But considering the risks as well helps prevent you from becoming overconfident. When your confidence is kept in check you will be in a far greater position to prepare for the worst occurring. Your confidence will be based more on rational, rather than wishful, thinking.

One of the biggest dangers of all is being blind to risks because of overconfidence. Overconfidence can cause you to lose touch with your inbuilt protector – FEAR. As one police officer told me, 'Overconfidence can get you hurt, because with overconfidence you don't get that fear you need to get you through.'

'You need to look at the "what ifs" and act on them before they happen.'

PAUL BRIGGS

Fear Professionals recognise the possibility of failure. This keeps expectations realistic and avoids the overconfidence trap.

'When riding 30-foot waves I use the saying, "Fear keeps you sane",' Layne Beachley explained. 'This means that you don't go out there thinking that you are invincible. Instead you go out there just a little afraid, knowing the ocean can take you whenever it's ready to. And life is like that.'

Jeff Fenech had firsthand experience of the price of overconfidence:

> 'The fights I lost, I knew that if it had been the young, hungry Jeff Fenech from the '80s, things would have been different. But I had success and I got carried away with it. I thought I was invincible and took short cuts. The moment you take things for granted you just change automatically, before you even know it's happening to you. It's then that you lose; you end up realising that we are all human, no bigger or better than anyone else. If you don't prepare properly and take short cuts, no matter what it is, then there will always be someone out there better than you.'

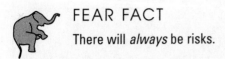

FEAR FACT

There will *always* be risks.

To expect there will be no risks when stepping out of your comfort zone is unrealistic. Fear Professionals accept the fact that there will always be risks. This allows them to be aware of two very important points. Firstly, the futility in waiting for risks to disappear before trying something new. And secondly, knowing the risks can reduce the likelihood of their occurring.

Gaby Kennard goes through each risk when she flies. She considers the risk and then the best way to handle it if it occurs.

> 'You have to be prepared for the worst otherwise you will be vulnerable. For example when flying I'm thinking, "If I had engine failure, where would I land?" When I'm flying across the ocean I'm looking at the swell. So if I have to crash-land I would go with the swell and land in the trough.'

If she panicked and landed in the swell, rather than going with it, the impact would be similar to driving into an oncoming truck. By thinking about the worst-case scenario, Gaby has armed herself in the best possible way.

So how do Fear Professionals consider the worst and still manage to remain confident? They assess the potential worst which prevents them from being flooded with panic. This is the third secret, which I have named Positive Pessimism.

Secret 3

POSITIVE PESSIMISM: PREPARE FOR THE
WORST WHILE EXPECTING THE BEST

The Fear Professionals' third secret, Positive Pessimism, involves considering the worst so that you can prepare for it happening. Positive Pessimism is similar to investing on the stock market with the positive outlook of making money coupled with the acceptance that you could lose money. In order for Positive Pessimism to work, there are two basic questions you need to ask yourself:

1. What is the worst?

2. Am I prepared to accept it?

These two questions are extremely powerful in helping you both to assess danger and to guard against becoming overconfident. Fear Professionals assess the risks associated with facing a situation and, if the risks are too high, they walk away. That's right, if the risks are more than what they are prepared to accept, they walk away. This sounds simple but does it actually work in situations you and I might face, especially when the situations are emotionally charged? The two simple questions of Positive Pessimism can be applied to your life decisions in the same way a Fear Professional would.

FEAR FACT

A pessimist complains about the rain.
An optimist expects the rain to stop.
A Positive Pessimist carries an umbrella.

★ QUESTION 1: WHAT IS THE WORST?

The first step is to accurately identify the worst. I say accurately because we have a tendency to either overestimate or underestimate the worst, all due to mismanaging fear. The fear you are likely to experience when you accurately consider the worst is often the biggest hurdle of all. This is because when you think about the worst, your mind will probably become overwhelmed by fear. This is perfectly normal and it's a fact that Fear Professionals have learned to accept.

Before Gaby Kennard considered where to crash-land, she first had to plan her quest, and consider the various worst-case scenarios involved:

> 'I was really scared when I first started to plan the trip because I had no idea if I could do it. First there was the fear of having no money. I had nothing. I mortgaged my house to finance the trip. Then I faced the fear of ridicule. Here is this woman who wants to fly around the world, and what if I fail? What if I can't get it together? So both my security and my reputation were on the line. Channel Nine agreed to sponsor me if they could have a camera in the cockpit filming me all the time. It was scary saying to Channel Nine, "Yes, I am going to do this and that." And it was scary knowing I'd be filmed. It was absolutely terrifying to make this commitment to the trip and then have the media write stories promoting me.'

Risks that scare us do so for our own safety. If we really think about them, we are more likely to take them seriously and limit their potential threat. Pat, a working mother, would leave her two-month-old baby in the car while she went inside the station to pay for petrol. Her gut feeling told her it wasn't right to leave her baby unattended, but she convinced herself that everything would be fine. After all, she was only leaving her baby in the car for a short moment, and it would save her a lot of time. Then Pat had a dream that she went to pay for the petrol when an armed hold-up was in progress. There was terror in Pat's voice as she re-called the dream and explained how the gunman screamed at her to lay face-down on the floor. As she lay there, she realised that her baby was in a hot car and it was nearly feeding time. Even though it was just a dream, Pat said she would never leave her baby alone in the car again. Why? She had considered the worst and the fear she associated with leaving her baby in the car made her view the risks far more seriously.

Fear Professionals handle their fear so that it does not over-whelm them or their ability to accurately consider the worst. How? Step one of the Fear Finder: acknowledging and ac-cepting fear as normal – that's it! When considering the worst, acknowledge your fear and its effect on you. This allows you to view the situation objectively. Know what is the worst before stepping out of a comfort zone.

★ QUESTION 2: AM I PREPARED TO ACCEPT THE WORST?

So you've identified the worst and reduced the risks as much as is in your control. Now it's time to use Positive Pessimism's second question, 'Am I prepared to accept the worst?' Answering the second question requires you to consciously remove those rose-tinted glasses and see the situation clearly, which is often more difficult than it seems.

Before the Fear Professionals taught me to accept the worst, I'd been a big advocate of ignoring risks among my family and friends – 'Don't say that, Grandma, you're not going to die,' or,

'Don't think about what you could lose on the stock market, think of what you could gain.'

My family and I encouraged my brother to start his own business but not to identify the possible risks. We all reasoned that his product was a certain winner, so why be negative and think about the worst? Better to think like a winner. My brother took our advice, ignored the worst and jumped in the deep end. He ended up losing a lot of money as a result. If he had considered the worst beforehand, he may not have taken such huge risks.

Wayne Bennett said, 'There is a price for everything we choose in life. You have to ask yourself, "Am I prepared to live with the price I have to pay?"' This philosophy can be applied to any choice involving risk. Are you prepared to buy a second-hand electrical item knowing that, if there is anything wrong, you will not be able to take it back? Are you prepared to buy a car, without getting it checked, and risk it being a lemon? Are you prepared to leave your children with a babysitter you know little about?

If you answer yes, then you must be prepared to accept the consequences these risks present. Fully accepting the risks is the key here and not blissfully thinking, 'Sure there are risks, but they won't happen to me.' A formidable opponent in any field is one who has full knowledge of the consequences and is still prepared to face them in order to attain their goal.

**'How was I able to fight with broken hands?
It wasn't that I had a bigger heart than
anyone else, I had just prepared myself to
accept the worst.'**

JEFF FENECH

If you are not prepared to accept the worst your situation presents, what can you do to reduce the likelihood of it happening? I stress the word reduce, as eliminating the risks altogether is an impossible goal. A realistic aim is to reduce the severity or likelihood of the risks occurring.

★ REDUCING RISKS

After considering the worst and accepting it, you must reduce the risks to a level you feel comfortable with. How do Fear Professionals use Positive Pessimism to reduce the potential risks? They weigh up how easily they could deal with the risk and then compare this with the severity of the risk at hand. Dick Smith explains how he balances his pessimism with optimism when assessing the risks involved in an exploration adventure:

'I look at the negatives but I look at them as positives. That is what gives me the excitement to do it. Risk

Dick Smith after reaching the North Pole. (Photo: Dick Smith)

management is quite an art, and I have done some risky adventures and I have never yet hurt myself or even put a dent on an aeroplane in my adventures. This is all because a lot of work has been spent on risk management.

'When I go into a new situation, I assess the whole thing. I write down everything that can go wrong and then I work out how am I going to manage that and how am I going to reduce the chance of that happening. So even when I fly around the world in a single-engine helicopter, I have a very good life raft; I have a very good survival beacon. So if I come down in the water, I believe that I will be able to get out and get into my life raft and someone will be able to recover me.'

Dick Smith is a classic example of what being a Positive Pessimist is all about. He uses his pessimism to acknowledge the potential risks, writing down everything that could go wrong. Then he reduces the likelihood of the worst happening and prepares for the worst-case scenario as well. Once he has reduced the risks as much as is in his control, he then, and only then, asks himself if he is prepared to accept the risks.

How can we apply Dick's approach? Find an issue that has been on your mind. It may be something like:

- having a full medical check-up
- getting a pet for the kids
- writing up your will and deciding who to include in it
- buying an electrical appliance without knowing which brand or model is best for you.

Whatever your issue is, once you have it in your mind, decide what the worst consequence is if you proceed. Can you handle it if the worst happens? If you can, great. Now what can you do to reduce the likelihood of the worst happening? Think about practical ways – they may be small – to make the situation a little friendlier.

A friend of mine, Matt, wanted to buy the house of his dreams, but it meant getting into high debt. With his income, Matt could afford to make the repayments, but only just. He worried that there would never be another house quite like it and was afraid that someone else would buy it if he didn't sign straightaway.

Often when it is something we desperately want, we're far more vulnerable to ignoring risks so we can collect the prize. And it's easy to get swept up in the moment. In the case of buying a house that's just beyond the budget, what could be the potential worst? Consider the unexpected expenses of finding out the house needs more work, of getting unforeseen car or medical bills, losing your job, or simply a rise in interest rates. Buying a house is full of potential risks and to expect to get rid of the risks altogether is wishful thinking. Matt should explore ways of reducing the chance of the risks occurring. Ways of doing this could be:

- getting professional financial and legal advice

- taking into account interest rate rises when considering what he can afford to borrow

- having the property inspected

- reviewing his living costs – is there margin for unexpected expenses?

'You must have back-up plans. If you go in blind in any situation, you are going to get hurt.'

ROD WATERHOUSE

The job interview is another area that raises fears for many people. Applying Positive Pessimism may include preparing for difficult questions. Here are a few suggestions to reduce the risk of the worst happening:

- Find out all you can about the position and/or company.
- Read books on successful job interviews.
- Ask people working within similar industries for advice.

Once you have done all you can to reduce the risks, in this case handling difficult interview questions, you can remain positive and focus on attaining your goal.

You can reduce risks by preparing for the worst and be in a much stronger position to accept the worst in the case of it happening. But what if you cannot adequately reduce the risks and are unsure about accepting the worst? Do not proceed. Even Fear Professionals say no to opportunities that they assess as too risky.

★ CAUTION BEFORE COURAGE

Fear Professionals are a very cautious group of people who are not interested in facing a fear just to be rid of it. They are able to face dangerous situations frequently because they are not afraid to walk away from a challenge. When a Fear Professional cannot reduce the risks to a level that they feel is suitable, whether it be due to physical limitations or factors outside their control, they say no. Fear Professionals know the importance of honestly acknowledging their limitations when considering the worst.

'I never put myself in a position where there is no exit.'
FRONT-LINE POLICE OFFICER

Tony Gasser Jnr had to give up working with lions when he considered the risks insurmountable.

'I stopped working with the lions because in Australia it became nearly impossible to find lions that wouldn't be too dangerous for training. In the early days, Australia had all the lion parks and lion safaris, and there were plenty of animals bred in captivity. The problem of no longer having these good blood lines is that the lions go back to being very pure, with their natural jungle instincts. When this happens, it becomes far too dangerous to work with them. I'd been noticing dangerous things happening where a lot of lion trainers were getting hurt. So I decided, "Okay, I know what I know and I shouldn't take the risk working with lions that are unsuitable to be trained, because an animal is only as good as the animal is."'

Even though he was well equipped to handle the lions before, the risks became too great for Tony. He was not able to meet the new risks and was not willing to accept the worst-case scenario, which left him with one option: not to proceed.

Knowing when to walk away from risks that are too high takes tremendous honesty and courage. It requires you to examine your strengths and weaknesses with equal weighting. Generally people prefer to focus solely on either their weaknesses or their strengths. As one police officer explained, 'Before facing a dangerous situation you have to be brutally honest with yourself about what you can and cannot do.'

Alan Jones was adamant about this topic:

'You'll never handle fear if your expectation exceeds your ability. There's no use saying that you can stand on [stage in] the concert hall of the Opera House and sing the leading aria from *La Traviata* if you can't sing. In other words, face reality. Admit your limitations! That doesn't mean you won't be able to triumph over them. Where expectation and reality are about equal, there is this legitimate fear of "I have now got to deliver." There has got to be a sense of realism otherwise you're kidding yourself.'

Joe Bugner understood this when he came up against Muhammad Ali in the boxing ring. 'To pretend to be an Ali beater would have been an absolute farce. I knew that Ali was one of the greatest boxers that I had ever confronted in the boxing ring. I feel the reason both our fights went the distance, compared to most fighters he knocked out, was because I was aware of my limitations and didn't pretend to be someone I wasn't.' Ali beat Joe in both their contests, but it was an achievement for Joe to go the distance. 'It's all about knowing your limitations, knowing where your strengths and weaknesses are, because when you know this then you're more likely able to control your fear and succeed.'

> **'If you haven't got the tools to do a job then it is better to back down and come back later once you have them.'**
> NEIL SONTER

Acknowledging your limitations will help you assess risks and know when to walk away from a situation that is out of your league. Make no mistake, I'm not saying that you should use your limitations as a scapegoat for avoiding new challenges. Accept new challenges, but only when they are the right challenges at the right time. When you know your limitations you can still address the

Jim Cassidy winning the Golden Slipper. (Photo: Steve Hart Photographics)

risks associated with a situation. This can be achieved either directly or indirectly. For example, you may directly reduce the risks by gaining more knowledge of the situation so you can return at a later date. In this way you are building your strengths by working on your limitations. You may instead choose to indirectly overcome the risks by walking away from a situation in which you feel dangerously limited and concentrating on areas that better suit your strengths. Such was the case with Jim 'Pumper' Cassidy, who dreamed of playing rugby for the All Blacks but was too small physically to risk it. He assessed his limitations and redirected his focus to horse racing. By using his physical size to advantage, Jim is now hailed as one of Australia's most successful jockeys.

Remember, even though Fear Professionals look at their limitations and strengths with equal weight, it is their strengths that help them deal with their limitations. This is the best way of gauging whether the level of risk associated with a situation is acceptable or not.

What is an acceptable amount of risk? What a Fear Professional sees as an acceptable amount of risk may be different to what you and I think is acceptable. An acceptable level of risk is relative to the individual and the situation they are experiencing at the time. Fear Professionals have developed an elevated level of calmness when risks are high by taking smaller steps to build up their courage levels over time. If the risks are too high, then they walk away. These Fear Professionals are good role models if you ever feel inadequate for being cautious. It is this caution that protects Fear Professionals so that they can face risks on a consistent basis.

FEAR FACT
Positive Pessimism helps you recognise and deal with potential risks before they become an emergency.

★ WHAT IF YOU CANNOT WALK AWAY?

A public speaker's worst nightmare is someone from the audience asking a difficult question. I remember giving a talk on fear and someone in the audience asked a question that really challenged me. I had just mentioned that Fear Professionals walk away from risks that they can't reduce to an acceptable level, when a woman in the audience asked, 'What if you are in a situation that you cannot walk away from, like an unhappy relationship or job?'

When Fear Professionals are in situations they cannot walk away from they accept the dangers they can't control and instead focus on controlling their reaction to the situation. Gaby Kennard gave an excellent example. In her quest to be the first Australian woman to fly solo around the world, Gaby was caught in a thunderstorm. With bolts of lightning striking around her plane, it wasn't a situation she could walk away from.

> 'Really, it's more about acceptance. When I was flying through the storm I knew that as long as the engine was going and I did everything I could in my power to

control the situation, that was all I could do. And, if that wasn't good enough, then it was out of my hands and up to God as to what my fate would be. If a bolt of lightning came and blew my aeroplane up, then I accepted that that was the way it had to be. Once I accepted the worst possible scenario, it freed me to concentrate on that which was in my control, like flying the plane out of the storm.'

Accepting the worst in situations when there is no other solution can give you a powerful advantage. By knowing and then accepting that wherever lightning might strike was totally out of her hands, Gaby could concentrate on her reaction and fly out of the storm. By accepting the worst you are subtly preparing your mind in case the worst actually does happen. In this event, because you have envisaged the worst, it will be less of a shock. This gives you a better chance of managing your fear instead of being overwhelmed by it.

Would this confidence-building technique be of benefit in everyday life? The answer is a definite yes. Here are some stressful everyday situations that you may not be able to walk away from:

- Hating your job but not being able to leave due to financial commitments.
- Visiting difficult in-laws once a year.
- Feeling unhappy with your partner but mindful of your children's welfare.
- Driving an old car because you do not have the money to replace it.

Accepting the risks you cannot walk away from and refocusing on controlling your reaction to the situation is very empowering. The story of Veronica, a client of mine, is a classic example of this.

Veronica was stuck in a job she didn't like. The job wasn't challenging, customers complained, and the boss was rude. But Veronica had financial commitments, and leaving without a new job wasn't an option. What did she do? She focused on controlling her own reaction. She looked for new opportunities but tried to be upbeat in her current job. If she was going to be stuck there until she found a better job, she would at least have a say in how she responded to her work environment. Both customers and staff commented on Veronica's positive manner and, after a while, one of her customers was so impressed that he offered her a job with better conditions.

Recapping on Positive Pessimism, it can be divided into three parts:

1. What is the worst-case scenario?

2. Do you accept the worst-case scenario?

   • If an honest yes, then go for it.

   • If no, then what can you do to reduce the risks?

   • If no, and you can't reduce the risks, then walk away.

3. If you cannot walk away, then accept the risks and focus on what you can control, like your own reaction to the situation.

EXERCISE

The next time you're faced with a risk, ask yourself what the worst consequence would be and if you are prepared to accept it. Whether it is driving without insurance or buying something on impulse, try to use Positive Pessimism in your day-to-day life.

CHAPTER SUMMARY

IN THIS CHAPTER YOU LEARNED:

1. Considering the worst increases confidence and reduces the likelihood of the worst happening by alerting you to the risks.

2. The Fear Professionals' third secret – *Positive Pessimism: Prepare for the worst while expecting the best.*

3. Fear Professionals place caution before courage when determining whether to confront a fear.

4. The questions to ask yourself when facing a fearful situation: What is the worst? Am I prepared to accept it?

CHAPTER 4

Beating procrastination

'You have to want to face a fear. Whether it be because of a strong desire to improve yourself or an interest in the task at hand – if you don't have this need, you'll prevent yourself from facing it every time.'

Layne Beachley, six-time world surfing champion

'It doesn't matter what fear you are facing, before you do it, you have to ask yourself what your reason is for facing your fear in the first place.'

Johnny Lewis, boxing trainer of three world champions

Do you keep putting things off, moving them aside, reassigning them to another pile? Do these things then nag at you, bugging you to the point of distraction? You can put it off right until the last minute but you'll probably find yourself having to do it anyway. We postpone all sorts of things, big and small:

- Going to the dentist
- Meeting new people
- Doing tax returns
- Starting a diet
- Looking for a job
- Climbing up on the roof to unblock the gutters
- Becoming computer literate.

In this chapter you will learn a very common problem you're likely to share with Fear Professionals when facing a fearful situation. You will discover the Fear Professionals' fourth secret, which will help you develop the courage to face whatever you have been avoiding, unlocking your potential so you can step out of your comfort zone and try new things. You will learn to challenge the commonly held misconception that holds us back. The Fear Professionals will explain how they motivate themselves in their dangerous lines of work.

If you find it difficult to face fearful situations, rest assured you are not alone. Even though many of the Fear Professionals face threatening conditions on a regular basis, they still have immense difficulties. But if they've faced the fearful situation before, surely the Fear Professionals don't find it difficult the next time round? Once you face a fearful situation, the fear is gone, right? WRONG!

MYTH 4

IF YOU FACE YOUR FEAR, YOU'LL GET OVER IT.

Even with all their experience, Fear Professionals still don't want to face certain situations. This drive to avoid danger is a natural human instinct designed to protect. But many people believe that to get over a fear is easy, you just face it. The weakness of this belief is that it does little to provide motivation for leaving a comfort zone, and it is this motivation which is the corner-stone of courage.

Have you ever faced a fearful situation with little or no motivation to actually do it? Or have you faced a situation because someone was pushing you or saying that everything would be fine? Facing a situation when it is another's idea, when you can see no benefit in doing so, is dangerous because the motivation required to face the situation is the other person's, not yours. If you can't see the benefits in facing a situation, your motivation will be to avoid it.

What do I mean by not having motivation to face a fearful situation? Many people use the term 'procrastination' to describe this predicament. Think of a time that you avoided facing a fearful situation. Here are some examples to jog your memory:

- Remaining silent in a meeting instead of sharing your ideas.

- Rejecting an invitation to a social event because you might not know anyone.

- Avoiding a new activity only to regret it later.

Could you relate to any of these scenarios? Or did you come up with some of your own? If so, ask yourself the following question:

'How strong was my reason to complete the task?'

How strong was your reason to speak up in the meeting or to go to the party not knowing anyone? It is highly likely that you chose to avoid the situation because your reason not to face it was stronger than your reason to face it. Most people don't like to admit openly that their reason not to act was due to fear. As a result we develop excuses to mask our fears. Do any of these sound familiar?

- There's no point in speaking up about my idea because someone else has probably already thought of it.

- There's no point in going, it would probably be a boring party anyway.

- I just can't be bothered trying something new today.

'If someone says, "I can't do it", I ask them, "Can't do it or don't want to do it?"'

JIM CASSIDY

We all use these excuses to avoid leaving a comfort zone, because stepping out will feel uncomfortable and expose us to the unknown. So how do the Fear Professionals do it so regularly? They use the fourth secret. Without it, it's nearly impossible to face a fearful situation.

The fourth secret is a personalised empowering tool designed to help you beat procrastination and face a fearful situation. It's built on the concept that to face a fearful situation, you need motivation. Knowing what you will gain from facing your situation is the foundation.

Secret 4

YOU NEED A STRONG REASON TO FACE A
FEARFUL SITUATION

Fear Professionals know that to leave a comfort zone they need a strong reason to continue into potential danger. This motivation has to be stronger than the fear of facing the situation. If the fear is stronger than the reason, then avoidance, usually in the form of procrastination, is likely to set in. A Fear Professional focuses on this reason to give strength and courage.

Valerie Taylor's reason for diving with sharks is her photography. 'Most people when they dive are thinking, "Sharks! Sharks! Sharks!" The last thing I think about is sharks. My reason for being in there is to take photos and that is what I focus on.'

**'If you have a strong enough reason you
can do anything.'**

WAYNE BENNETT

Gaby Kennard's reasons were more emotional. After her husband left her, she fell into a depression. 'I felt I had to prove myself to myself by doing something very difficult and make it work or I was just going to be nothing and go slowly to my death.' She worried about leaving her kids, though, and about leaving them motherless should anything happen on the journey. 'Yet I felt that, in a strange way, my motivation was that I'd be a great role model for my kids and others who didn't want to be ordinarily normal either. I thought, "If I do this, then my kids would feel free in themselves to go for their dreams." I really believed that, and I think it was this strong belief that got me through it.'

The Fear Professionals know that it is vital to have a reason to face a fearful situation. But just what this reason is depends on the individual. For many of the police officers interviewed, the reason was that they felt it to be their job to uphold the law at all costs. For Jeff Fenech, the reason was to avoid greater pain later on. This reason was strong enough to counter broken hands in one world title.

'I knew that the fights I had lined up were once-in-a-lifetime opportunities for me to prove myself to myself. If I pulled out because of my hands, the regret would have been something I could never have lived with. So for me, the motivation to win and be the best I could was stronger than the pain in my hands.'

Jeff Fenech's motivation to win was stronger than the pain of his broken hands. (Photo: David Mahony, courtesy the National Library of Australia)

Jeff's story is not to encourage you to ignore physical pain to attain a goal. Pain, like fear, is there to warn us of danger. But his victory was the result of having a strong reason to face a fearful situation. Added to Jeff's motivation was his general reason to succeed – to make life easier financially. Kostya Tszyu had similar reasons, as trainer Johnny Lewis discovered. 'You've got to have a reason to be the best because talent alone won't get you there. Kosyta Tszyu came from Russia with only a bag of clothes. Jeff Fenech's parents were migrants to Australia who were doing it tough with a big family. So both Kostya and Jeff had a tremendous hunger to prove themselves and make life better for themselves and their families. And I think it was this reason of them wanting to succeed that has made them both as successful as they are.'

'If you have no desire or interest to confront a fear, then why do it?'

LAYNE BEACHLEY

Fear Professionals described a broad range of reasons motivating them to face fearful situations:

- Loyalty to work colleagues and friends.
- A duty to protect the innocent.
- A deep desire to attain a personal goal.
- The need to be unique and not follow the crowd.

Having a strong reason can be applied to any fearful situation. When you start to tailor a reason to fit your own circumstances, you will realise that having a strong reason really does work.

★ STRONG REASONS – HOW DO THEY WORK?

Why is it so important to have a strong reason to face a fearful situation? A strong reason reassures your mind of the possible benefits of engaging in a fearful situation. The mind naturally wants to focus on the outcome of a situation. When you do not provide your mind with a preferred outcome, it will waver between possible risks and rewards, with the tendency to focus on the worst as a natural safety mechanism. When your mind focuses only on the worst-case scenario, it concludes that, if there is nothing to gain from facing a fearful situation, why face it at all? A strong reason gets your mind on side by focusing on the possible benefits of engaging in a fearful situation.

Be aware that having a strong reason does not stop you from feeling fear. You will most probably still feel fear, but it will not cripple you because you now know that fear is power.

FEAR FACT

It's not how you do it but why you do it that gives empowerment.

★ FINDING A REASON

How do you find a positive, powerful reason that allows you to beat procrastination and face your fearful situation? Start by asking yourself the following question:

'What can I gain by facing my fearful situation?'

A Fear Professional knows that there is no point in facing a fearful situation unless there is something to be gained. Without this awareness of potential gain, confidence levels would drop. Knowing what can be gained by facing your fearful situation gives your mind a goal to focus on: your reward.

**'Having ability is only part of it. You have
to have "the want" to face a challenge.
That is the key.'**

DAVID GRAINGER

Here are just a few possible gains resulting from facing a fearful situation:

- Money in the bank
- A better sex life
- A promotion at work.

The next step is to know the types of deception used by procrastination to prevent you from leaving a comfort zone.

★ SOLVE THE DECEPTIONS OF PROCRASTINATION

Procrastination's sole aim is to keep you in a comfort zone, where fear can still control you. Recognising the signs of procrastination in your life will help you defeat it.

Deception 1: No decision is better than the wrong decision

Adam wants the book that he lent to Jess, but he doesn't want to ask her for it. He's stuck between wanting his book back and facing an awkward moment with Jess, so he does nothing at all.

Have you ever experienced a time when you wanted to step out of a comfort zone but the more you thought about it, the more unsure you became as to whether it was a good idea? Indecision is the lifeblood of procrastination. When you cannot make up your mind and become frozen on the potential risks, procrastination has won again.

Solution: Make a decision – Indecision is all about thinking too much and not acting. The fastest way to build a bridge over this is to make a decision. Remember, procrastination doesn't want you to make a decision because then it can keep you imprisoned in your comfort zone. To avoid fixating on the risks and not acting at all, use chapter 3's Positive Pessimism to weigh up the risks and the gains. Then make a decision and act on it. Making a decision – often any decision – is better than no decision. If your mind is toying between two options, then perhaps the costs and benefits are equal. Stop procrastination in its tracks by making a decision and then acting on it.

Deception 2: The first step has to be huge

How often have you made up your mind to step out of a comfort zone but, when it came to taking that first step, it seemed too big to take at that point in time? Procrastination will try to deceive you that the first step out of a comfort zone has to be superhuman. This will ensure that you stay imprisoned within your comfort zone where procrastination can limit your actions and control you.

Solution: Take small steps – You can beat procrastination by taking a much smaller step out of your comfort zone. To achieve this, use Fear Training, as outlined in chapter 2. If your goal is to join a gym, for instance, but the time commitment and the joining process seem too daunting, try a fifteen-minute jog around the block instead. It may not be as 'worthy' as an hour-long class, but it will be better than sitting on the couch, which is where you'll end up when you put off the gym until another day.

Procrastination will try to convince you that taking such a small step out of your comfort zone is a waste of time and won't achieve a thing. This is why taking the first step out of a comfort zone is so hard. But once you have taken that first small step, you've beaten procrastination, so your next step will be easier again. Go on, take that first step out of your comfort zone by making it a small one.

FEAR FACT
Small steps create motivation.

Making a decision and then acting on it by taking small steps are the two tools to beating procrastination. To practise, start by choosing a situation you've been avoiding. Once you have this situation in mind, decide on an action and break it down into smaller steps, if necessary. Then do it.

> **'Someone who is potentially dangerous is a person in control of their temper and has a clear motive for their actions.'**
> FRONT-LINE POLICE OFFICER

★ EMOTIONAL REASONS ARE POWERFUL ONES

Another method Fear Professionals use to beat procrastination is to make their reason highly emotional. What does this mean? If your reason is backed by strong feelings, it becomes far more powerful. A passionate reason has your heart and soul working with your mind – nothing could stop you!

My most pressing need for an emotional reason came in my teens, when I went on an exchange program to Honduras. Disaster struck when my lung collapsed and I had to undergo an emergency operation without anaesthetic. Being hospitalised for four weeks in a third-world country was a life-changing experience – I was in constant pain, with a tube sewn crudely into my chest and instructions not to move an inch or I could die. This led to painful bedsores on my back, and I suffered from depression, exhaustion and dangerously low body weight, all without anyone familiar beside me. At my lowest point I wanted to die just to be free of the nightmare, and I realised I needed an emotionally charged reason to stay alive. My reason was to make it home so I could see my family again. I imagined the heartache they'd experience if I were sent back in a casket. This was reason enough to stay strong and withstand the distressing situation I found myself in.

FEAR FACT
Emotion beats procrastination.

★ IF NO GAIN, THEN WHAT?

What happens if you cannot think of any gain that could come from facing your fearful situation? If this is the case, it's likely that you are better off walking away from your fearful situation. If you cannot see any gain, your body's natural safety mechanism will try to stop you every time. Remember, when a Fear Professional cannot see any gain from facing a fearful situation, they do not face it.

Elite athletes are able to make lifestyle sacrifices and train to the point of pain to achieve their goals. But there comes a time when an athlete needs to revisit their reason to train, as Tony O'Loughlin, a respected and experienced boxing trainer, explained:

> 'It is very important for an athlete to have the courage and determination to be able to face the fears and stress of competing at an elite level. However, it's just as important for them to acknowledge when they are no longer physically and mentally able to stay at that level and instead

have the courage to say, "That's it, no more." They have to know when enough is enough and walk away, otherwise the risk of serious injury is a very real possibility.'

Stephen Gall's initial reason to race in motor sports was later outweighed by reasons to stop. 'One of the reasons I loved racing at high speeds was because the adrenaline rush was amazing. I miss it now but it became far more important to me to stay healthy to be there for my family.'

Stephen's example is a strong one: walk away from a fearful situation when you feel the risks outweigh the gains. This is different from the effect of procrastination, which entices you to stay in your comfort zone. Many people find this difficult to distinguish and they feel guilty or weak for walking away from a fearful situation. Remember, there is an important difference between not doing something that may harm you and not doing something that may strengthen you.

Stephen Gall leading the pack in a recent motocross race. (Photo: Mark Austin)

Whatever your reason to leave a comfort zone, if it contains emotion and focuses on gain, then it is likely to motivate you. Unhelpful types of reasons should be avoided.

 FEAR FACT

No reason to stay, then walk away.

★ UNHELPFUL REASONS: SOMEONE ELSE'S REASON

Do not use someone else's reason when you do not want to. When well-meaning friends, family or acquaintances try to convince you to face a fearful situation but you can't see any benefit in facing it, then their reason is not your reason. Your mind will be more focused on escaping the situation without harm instead of facing it to the best of your ability. When friends drag you on stage to sing at a karaoke bar or push you into abseiling down a cliff, consider whether you'd be doing it for their reason or yours.

Do any of these sound familiar?

- Go on, just do it!

- What doesn't kill you makes you stronger.

- If you don't do it, you will always regret it.

- If you run from this fear, you will run from every other fear you face.

'Whatever your cause is, make sure you fight for your reasons and not someone else's.'
JOSH CLEMSHAW

It's fine to use someone else's reason if you agree with it and, therefore, adopt it as your own. If you're standing at the top of that cliff and you think, 'Actually, yes, if I run from this, I will run from everything else, and this will help me prove something to myself,' then use that reason. But if you're thinking, 'Just because I choose not to abseil doesn't mean that I will run from other fears – I hate abseiling,' then it's not your reason. It's theirs. And be warned, using someone else's reason to face a fearful situation, one you do not support, can be potentially dangerous. If the person really pushes you to adopt their reason, then how to handle it is discussed in more detail in chapter 6. For now, remember it is vital for your reason to be one you believe in not one that will keep others happy.

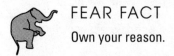

FEAR FACT
Own your reason.

When used correctly, having a strong reason to step out of a comfort zone is a fantastic way of motivating you to face situations you would otherwise have avoided. The benefits of this are endless – experiencing new things, meeting new people, making more money.

EXERCISE

Think of something you have always avoided. Ask yourself, 'What are the benefits of facing it?' Write these down. If you truly want these benefits, focusing on them will give you the motivation to stop procrastinating.

CHAPTER SUMMARY

IN THIS CHAPTER YOU LEARNED:

1. You can't get over a fear just by facing it.

2. The Fear Professionals' fourth secret – *You need a strong reason to face a fearful situation.*

3. A reason that is emotionally charged will provide powerful motivation, regardless of the dangers.

4. If there is no reason to stay, then walk away.

5. Positive Pessimism should be used to assess the potential risks of a situation.

CHAPTER 5

Share your fear

'When the act was on I always had capable people standing outside the cage. They were the eyes for my back.'

Tony Gasser Jnr, former world's youngest lion tamer

'You want friends that are solid, not ones that will bet each way on you.'

Jim Cassidy, winning jockey of two Melbourne Cups

Do you feel that fear is something only you can fix and you should, therefore, keep it to yourself?

A member of the elite Tactical Response Group (highly trained police working in the areas of siege and terrorist situations) explained the importance of sharing his fear with fellow officers:

> 'In the TRG we never went into a situation alone, we always went in as a group. Knowing that when I went into a situation, I wouldn't have to watch my back gave an incredible sense of confidence. We knew we could rely on each other; we gained strength from each other. And because the job was scary – living on adrenaline and wondering if today was the day you were going to die – it really helped being able to talk about our fears with each other. My children were only young at the time and knowing each time I went out on a call my life

Special forces police officers rely heavily on support from each other. (Photo: Mike Combe, NSW Police Public Affairs)

could be taken, leaving them fatherless, was terrifying. Many of the other officers had similar fears, though because the TRG was renowned for its toughness, we had to keep up a front like we were fearless. We felt we couldn't talk about our fears to just anyone. But being able to share my fears with the other officers and know my fears were normal, I believe, kept me sane. It allowed me to control my fears instead of the other way around.'

Talking about your fear with someone you trust is important in controlling fear and maintaining your sanity. Many of us choose not to talk about our fear and keep it to ourselves instead. Is keeping fear to yourself, hoping you will know how to deal with it, something you do? Do you put up a tough front and tell others you're fine when, really, fear is hounding you? Would you like to be able to ask others for help when you need it?

In this chapter you will learn why a Fear Professional never faces a fearful situation alone. Discover why they call on the assistance of carefully selected people to help them manage their fear. Learn how sharing your fear with someone you trust can increase your confidence and wellbeing and uncover why most people do not talk about their fear with others. You will be introduced to the Fear Professionals' fifth secret and to the characteristics of a Fear Friend.

If you find it difficult to call on the assistance of others when managing your fear, then rest assured you are not alone. Many people feel the need to hide their fear from others, reasoning that they should be able to deal with it alone. Fear Professionals know that to avoid asking for help makes facing a scary situation even more difficult and, often, more dangerous. Fear Professionals avoid the 'go it alone' approach when dealing with fear. So what happens if a Fear Professional is unable to get help when they need it? Then the Fear Professional will not face their fearful situation alone; it is that simple.

But what about those Fear Professionals who did face their fearful situations alone? Aren't there an elite few who didn't need the assistance of others to help them manage fear? What about the lion tamer, the shark diving experts, the solo athletes, and even explorers like Dick Smith and Gaby Kennard? Surely these Fear Professionals faced their fears alone, right? WRONG!

MYTH 5

SUCCESSFUL PEOPLE FACE THEIR FEARS ALONE.

Every Fear Professional interviewed, without exception, had a strong support team helping them face their fear. Even though these teams are quite often inconspicuous, they are pivotal in helping bolster a Fear Professional's unusually high courage levels.

Tony Gasser Jnr always had a team of dependable people standing just outside the cage ready to come to his aid if the lions turned on him. 'If it came down to it and a lion had jumped on me and started to chew into me, there were measures they would take to protect me. I had a lot of faith in the people around me because we were a team. I knew that I was not on my own and this gave me extra confidence. It's the people around you who give you confidence.'

Ron and Valerie Taylor also had their support crew along for their dives, both above and below the surface. So too, the explorers, who always had a team on the ground monitoring them and giving support and advice, from weather reports to possible landing sites. Gaby Kennard's ground crew even obtained last-minute security authorisation, ensuring she was not shot down

Gaby Kennard with ground crew preparing for her solo journey. (Photo: Sheri Forbes)

in a prohibited flight zone in Saudi Arabia.

All these Fear Professionals need their teams. Steve Van Zwieten explained why: 'If you get things right through teamwork, situations don't develop where anyone would have to choose between flight and fight.'

FEAR FACT

Fear Professionals choose not to face fearful situations alone.

Fear Professionals are adamant about sharing their fear with trusted others. But how does this apply to you? After all, Fear Professionals encounter life-threatening situations that are unlikely

Steve Van Zwieten shows his surveillance system comprising over 300 cameras, 625 times more powerful than the average home computer. This system becomes the security staff's eyes for their backs.

to apply to you or me. How could sharing your fear benefit you in day-to-day scenarios?

Here are just a few examples of when you could boost your courage levels by talking with someone you trust:

- Feeling nervous about an upcoming job interview

- Getting jitters before a driver's licence test

- Feeling apprehensive about marriage and kids

- Worrying that your relationship is losing its spark.

Talking with someone you trust about your fear can help relieve stress. One of the main reasons a person comes to a psychologist or therapist is to seek reassurance that they're not going crazy. If sharing your fear with trusted others is so empowering, why do we choose to keep our worries to ourselves?

'We all get scared, but it's how you react to fear that counts.'

TROY WATERS

★ WHY DO WE AVOID TALKING ABOUT OUR FEARS?

Western society has moved further away from the supportive community life of our ancestors and has instead focused more on being competitive individuals. We have learned to isolate ourselves and keep our fears to ourselves. This is done to avoid the appearance of weakness and to promote our highly prized individuality.

Melanie is a young woman who was suffering from depression. After talking with me for a while, she hesitantly referred to her relationship with her boyfriend. It turned out he was quite violent. On several occasions he had punched Melanie in the face, leaving visible bruising. She had covered up her boyfriend's violent actions by explaining to family and friends that she'd just fallen over.

After I told Melanie these actions were both domestic violence and a criminal offence, she seemed shocked and then relieved. She'd been bottling up her fear in the relationship by thinking the problem was her fault and that she had to somehow fix it herself. This only fuelled her depression. Once Melanie had shared her fear with me, she gradually felt more empowered to share it with others too, such as her family, friends and eventually the police.

Melanie is not alone in her resistance to sharing her fear with others. It's a common problem with most people. Because we're unwilling to share fear with others, we rely more and more on self-help for the answers. Yet people often misinterpret the self-help remedy, thinking they must manage and then face their fear unassisted, otherwise it is not 'self' help. But often when someone buries their fear, preventing it from being shared, fear will rear its head in other ways, like the depression in Melanie's case.

Fear Professionals know that, in their line of work, keeping fear to themselves can be life-threatening. Wisdom and strength can be gained through advice and support. Be aware of what's stopping you from sharing your fear.

★ FAMILY INFLUENCE

One of the biggest stumbling blocks you may face in sharing your fears is the influence your upbringing has had on you. If you were raised in an environment where talking about feelings was frowned upon, then this may cause you to put up a barrier between yourself and others. Can you relate to any of these influences that may prevent you from talking to others about your fear?

- Your parents did not talk openly about issues that concerned you.

- You had regular family moves as a child and learned not to get too close to people.

- You were over-protected and taught to see the world as unsafe.

- You were taught that making mistakes was bad.

- You were teased as a child and learned not to give people unnecessary ammunition.

Exploring the past and the possible source of not wanting to talk about feelings is empowering for one important reason: it highlights that your behaviour is learned. Therefore it can be un-learned through repeated practice of the behaviour that you want.

Practise taking small steps using the Fear Training in chapter 2 and share smaller fears with people you trust. That way, as you feel more comfortable, you can build up to sharing your larger fears. Once again, make sure you share your fears with someone you can trust. We'll go into more detail about Fear Friends later in the chapter. But for now it's important to know that just as family influence can act as a barrier to sharing your fear, so too can sharing your fear with the wrong person.

★ FRIENDLY HARMFUL ADVICE

It can be awkward when we pluck up the courage to voice our concerns with friends and family. This awkwardness is often compounded by others not knowing how to respond. Many people want to fix things and make the person better instead of just listening to their worries. One of the most common and destructive pieces of advice a person can give is the platitude, 'Just remember, there are people worse off than you.' It's as if this magical piece of advice will make you suddenly forget your concerns. Knowing that there are people 'worse off than you' implies that your fear is not warranted, which in turn implies that you're simply complaining. This is hardly a conducive environment for sharing. So you are left alone with your fear again.

> **'Assess your fear: is it irrational or is it justified? The media live on fear so it is easy to get swept away with the herd mentality.'**
>
> NEVILLE KENNARD

Unsuccessful attempts at sharing your fear can act as a barrier, preventing you from ever wanting to talk to others about your fear again. But it is vital not to let another person's poor management of your fear put you off ever sharing again. If there were only one practice to help maintain your mental health, it would be talking with a trusted person about your pressing worries. This is a basic strategy Fear Professionals use to take care of themselves and keep them thinking clearly when facing challenging situations.

This leads us to the Fear Professionals' fifth secret, enlisting the assistance of others to help you harness your fear.

Secret 5

SHARE YOUR FEARS

There's nothing truer than the age-old saying that 'a problem shared is a problem halved', especially when applied to fear. The simplicity of sharing your fear with someone you trust makes it accessible and effective.

Alan Jones tried to teach this to his ten-year-old godson, Daine. Daine was about to play in his first grand final and was incredibly nervous, so much so that he wouldn't have slept the night before. Alan noticed these nerves and asked him about them. When Daine admitted quietly that yes, he was nervous, Alan told him that he was just as nervous about it as a spectator. 'Suddenly Daine thinks, "Well there's nothing wrong with me being nervous because Alan is nervous too, and he has coached for Australia." And, in that way, some of the pressure has been taken away because I shared his fear with him. You have got to take the emotion out of the fearful situation by sharing it.'

Sharing your fear with someone you trust is empowering because it releases the tension of trying to keep your worries hidden. By sharing your fear with someone you trust, your worrying thoughts are verbalised, which allows you to see them in a completely different light. I'm always amazed at how many clients, while telling me of their worries, will suddenly sit bolt upright and have the solution to their problem.

'If I have doubts or worries about certain things then I talk to other people about it. It helps put my mind at ease.'

JUSTIN ROWSELL

Saying a problem out loud allows you to express the issue and hear it in a different form. There is still much debate as to how this benefits people but many believe that hearing the problem audibly instead of through internal monologue helps the brain interpret the information differently. This can often lead to a different solution.

★ SCARED TO TALK FEAR

The biggest challenge you're likely to face when sharing your fear is feeling scared to actually share it. It's ironic that we feel scared to talk about our fear with others. But it's a common response to the unwritten rule that only the weak feel fear and sharing it makes you appear vulnerable. As one Fear Professional, a coach, told me, 'Often athletes have this misconception that if they want to be at the top they must not feel fear or it will be perceived as a weakness. Bottling up fears because of being scared to share them is the best guarantee of self-destruction I know.'

It is perfectly normal to feel uncomfortable about sharing your fear, even with someone you trust. Many of my clients have said how difficult they initially found it to tell me about their concerns, worrying that I would judge them abnormal. Once these clients did share their fear, they expressed a tremendous sense of relief. The empowering feeling it gave was totally different to the expectations they had about sharing their concerns.

To take the first step toward sharing your fear with someone, use what you have learned from the last four chapters.

1. Acknowledge your fear, as discussed in chapter 1, which will bring it out into the open and allow you to embrace it.

2. Keep in mind the advice from chapter 2 and learn to control your own reaction by slowly approaching your fearful situation in steps you can manage. You may want to

tell a trusted person your fear over the phone or by email instead of face to face, or tell them a smaller fear first.

3. Use Positive Pessimism from chapter 3 to help you gauge the trustworthiness of the person you want to tell and consider the potential negative consequences of doing so. (Generally your intuition will tell you if the person is trustworthy or not, which is discussed in chapter 9.)

4. Finally, develop a strong reason to face your fearful situation, as outlined in chapter 4, and focus on your emotionally charged reason to give you the courage to actually share your fear. Your reason for sharing may be that you need assistance to attain a goal, like going for a job interview or buying the right car. Likewise, your reason to share fear may simply be to stop the mental anguish of holding it all in. Disclosure will empower you to face your fear.

★ SHARING FEAR DURING A FEARFUL SITUATION

Sharing your fear can be done in other ways, not just verbally. Fear can be shared physically by having the person you trust by your side to support you in the fearful situation. Just knowing that you will not be alone can increase confidence.

Gaby Kennard had one flight that was made easier by the presence of her fellow pilot at the time:

'I remember flying with Dick Smith and we were coming out of rough terrain in Colorado, which is very high mountainous country. It's always scary flying in an area you're unsure about. I looked at Dick and I knew that he was like me in that he was very nervous and apprehensive. So I thought, "Gosh, here is a guy who is a very experienced pilot, who's done a huge amount of

Dick Smith and
Gaby Kennard.

flying, and he feels fear like me." But he is a brilliant pilot
and he doesn't let his fear influence him negatively. He
seemed to use his fear positively. In this regard I learned
a lot by watching him.'

Gaby was able to draw confidence from Dick without saying
a word. Fear Professionals draw strength from the support people
they have around them. Having an extra pair of eyes looking out
for you, as the police officers all said, gives 'an incredible sense of
confidence'.

Think back to your own experiences of facing a fearful situation alone. Was the terror amplified because no one was by your
side? Take the example of going to a social event by yourself and
not knowing anyone there. Such a situation can produce fear in
even the most seasoned socialite. Now imagine going to that
same event with a friend or partner. Chances are your worries
will be dramatically reduced now that you are not alone. Why is
this? Having someone to go to the party with suddenly means
your fear is being shared.

> **'When competing, fear is a big factor for any athlete and a good trainer helps them manage it. Getting others' support when managing fear is crucial.'**
>
> TONY O'LOUGHLIN

Here are some examples of sharing your fear:

- Taking a friend with you to make a large purchase to reduce the fear of being manipulated into buying.

- Taking a friend for support when going to see a counsellor for the first time.

- Travelling with someone if you have a fear of flying. Telling the cabin crew about your fear can also help.

So what can you expect to gain by sharing your fear with someone you trust? You will increase your confidence, knowing that you are no longer alone with your fear. Your mind will see your concern differently when hearing it out loud. You will have an extra set of eyes looking for possible solutions to your problem. Finally, and most importantly, you will be able to relieve your fear by having shared it with your Fear Friend. This is one of the best ways to help ensure good mental health.

★ IDENTIFYING A FEAR FRIEND

A Fear Friend supports instead of rescues when fear is present. Rescuing, often the tactic employed by a caring friend, can be harmful when managing fear. Relying on another person to manage your fear for you only makes things harder. Remember, all you have full control over is yourself and, if you give this control up to someone else, you become helpless. The distinction between an unhelpful friend and a Fear Friend is comparable to that between an average coach and a good coach. An average coach often carries an athlete through the bad times, whereas a good coach stands back and assists from a distance. Alan Jones offered an analogy to explain the subtlety of a good coach:

'The coach should be constantly there softening and lessening the fearful burdens for the athlete. Or, as I say, "A porter on the railway station of life, there to help with the baggage." A good coach helps to lift the baggage. A good coach carries the athlete's baggage a little, reduces the load.'

Notice Alan said a good coach is like a porter. A porter does not take ownership of the baggage, they simply help carry it for the owner. A Fear Friend is not there to take ownership of your fears. Instead they, like the porter, are there to help you carry your fears. This is an important distinction to be aware of when looking for a suitable Fear Friend. You want someone who will support you in handling your fear, not rescue you from it. Often a friend who lacks this understanding will feel compelled to become a rescuer. Such a person will want to wrap you up in cotton wool, protecting and sheltering you from the dreaded fears of life. The mother who tries to protect her child from the everyday risks in life by doing everything for him is only depriving the child of learning to care for himself.

'To manage your fear you need to address it, share it and confront it.'

ALAN JONES

Remember, it is one thing to let someone help you carry your 'fear baggage' and quite another to allow another person to be in full control of it. You want a Fear Friend who will let you take ownership of your fear, and then be there to assist you if you need help.

FEAR FACT

A Fear Friend supports instead of rescues.

EXERCISE

Who can you share your fear with today? Start by sharing a small fear with someone you trust. Go on, pick up the phone, write a letter, type an email or talk to your Fear Friend face to face and share your fear.

CHAPTER SUMMARY

IN THIS CHAPTER YOU LEARNED:

1. Fear Professionals choose not to face fearful situations alone and instead seek the assistance of others to support them.

2. The Fear Professionals' fifth secret – *Share your fear*.

3. Sharing your fear by talking out loud with trusted others increases confidence, gets things off your chest and helps you to find solutions to your problems.

4. It is perfectly normal to feel a degree of apprehension when sharing your fear with someone you trust.

5. A Fear Friend supports instead of rescues.

CHAPTER 6

End a bully's Mind Games

'Muhammad Ali told me a long time ago, "When in doubt I go out and attack verbally." He would attack his opponents, scream at them and abuse them before the fight. And that was the only way he said he could cover his fear."

Joe Bugner, former world heavyweight boxing champion

'Quite often, if people or animals know we are scared, they will have fun at our expense.'

Valerie Taylor, shark diving expert

Have you ever tried ignoring a bully only to find it didn't work? We are often led to believe that the most effective way to stop a bully is to ignore them. Why is this rarely the case? Joe Bugner recalled an encounter with Muhammad Ali during their first fight in 1973:

> 'Although we knew each other and were sort of friends, when that bell went, man, was he awesome. There was no friendship there. Ali became the machine, the athlete that just wanted to get you out of the way. It was scary. Ali was very good at playing tricks with people's minds. Right before the start of our first fight he started yelling, "Bugner, you called me a nigger! You called me a nigger! No one, no one calls me a nigger! I'll fix you, boy."
>
> 'I never did call Ali this but he was able to stir the pot and, once he said it, I could not deny it because who was going to believe me. So there I was, standing in the ring with all these black Americans in the audience looking at me wanting to kill me. It was scary and I jumped on the spot so no one would see my knees shaking.
>
> 'Later on it became common knowledge that Ali used these tactics on several other fighters, including other black fighters.'

Joe Bugner poses with Muhammad Ali for pre-fight photos.
(Photo: AAP Image)

Bullying Mind Games, whether at home, school or in the workplace, are a source of fear hard to ignore. This is because they often occur in a closed situation where flight is not an option.

Do you regularly feel you are 'too nice' to say no? Do you want to ask for something but don't know how? Or have you been deliberately humiliated by another person in public or given in to a person's need to get their own way? Imagine the following scenario:

Janice is feeling great in her new outfit when she meets a group of friends. One of them says, 'You must work so hard because you always look really run down.' The entire group looks to Janice for her response to this disguised putdown. What can Janice say?

Welcome to the world of Mind Games! 'Mind Games' are the manipulative tricks bullies use on their victims. In this chapter you will learn how to identify different Mind Games and when someone is trying to bully you with them. You will discover why Fear Professionals avoid the common solution of ignoring Mind Games and how their sixth secret stops a bully in his tracks.

★ WHAT ARE MIND GAMES?

How would you react if a person insulted or belittled your child? Chances are you wouldn't allow it. And yet so often we let people walk all over us. One area of fear not normally discussed is how some people try to manipulate us by playing on our fears. Mind Games are emotional tricks a bully uses to manipulate you to do what they want. Sometimes these games are unintentional but often they are deliberate bullying. Mind Games can make you feel guilty, scared, humiliated or defensive. They are a form of intimidation so that you will do what the bully wants. They can be so powerful that often victims feel unable to do anything. Worst of all, bullying Mind Games often come from the people closest to us.

Fear Professionals are threatened by bullies' Mind Games on a regular basis. Boxers face the intimidation tactics of their opponents. Police officers deal with people trying to manipulate their way out of a speeding ticket. But if Fear Professionals face bullying Mind Games on such a regular basis, surely they would learn to ignore them, right? WRONG!

MYTH 6

IGNORING BULLYING WILL MAKE THE BULLY LEAVE YOU ALONE.

It's commonly believed that we should ignore the bullying Mind Games of others to make them stop. To protect us from taunts, we're encouraged as children to recite that 'Sticks and stones may break my bones but names will never hurt me'. But if these names really don't hurt, then why should we have to remember phrases to remind ourselves? Ignoring Mind Games is not the answer.

Just how common are Mind Games in everyday life? Here are some examples:

1. Tanya tells Fred that she doesn't have time to go to the movies. Fred acts depressed and gloomy but when she asks, he tells Tanya nothing is wrong.

2. Bonnie is concerned about the price of an alarm system. The saleswoman tells her, 'Yes, the alarm system is worth a lot of money, but is it worth more than your family's safety?'

3. Jim tells a group of friends that he is about to try a new sport. One friend says, 'If it's anything like the last time you tried something new, it should be good for a laugh.'

Fear Professionals know that trying to ignore Mind Games is like blowing on a fire to put it out – it will just burn brighter. Ignoring Mind Games empowers the bully for two reasons.

Firstly, what makes a bully's Mind Games so powerful is their secrecy. Victims often feel too scared to openly acknowledge a bully's Mind Games for fear of further attack. But when you say nothing, you are both strengthening and encouraging their use by keeping them hidden.

The second problem with trying to ignore hurtful Mind Games is that it's almost impossible to achieve. It's a bit like turning your back on a large wave and hoping that by ignoring it, the wave will go away. To put it another way, trying to ignore a bully's Mind Games is like trying to ignore a dripping tap. When you're not aware of the dripping, everything is fine. But the moment you become aware of the sound, you can't stop thinking about it. Mind Games are the same – to try to ignore them you first have to be aware of them. Once you have made yourself aware of a bully's Mind Games, they are difficult to ignore.

FEAR FACT

Ignoring Mind Games is difficult and can be harmful.

★ BE PREPARED TO STAND YOUR GROUND

If trying to ignore a bully's Mind Games only makes things worse, then what can you do? You will need to stand up to the bully. If you feel that this is beyond you, don't worry. By the end of this chapter, much of the mysticism surrounding bullies will be lifted so you will feel informed and empowered about how best to deal with them.

With that said, if thoughts of standing up to a bully still fill you with terror, rest assured that this is very normal. The majority of people feel this way about standing up to a bully. It is for this reason that for many people, the common response to a bully is comparable to that of seeing a shark while swimming – turning and fleeing. In the case of a shark, this can actually cause more trouble. Ron and Valerie Taylor explained that when most people see a shark in the water they react instinctively and try to outswim it. From a shark's perspective, though, a fleeing creature is potential prey. 'The normal reaction would be to run, but then you would be prey, because prey flees. An equal stands up to you. So you turn around, look the shark in the eye and hit it. You are its equal.'

The way most of us respond to a shark – fleeing – is often the same way we respond to a bully. Instead of standing up to the

Valerie Taylor patting a great white shark. (Photo: Ron and Valerie Taylor)

bully, we back down and say nothing. The problem is that when you say nothing, you are in effect acting like prey and leaving yourself vulnerable to further attack.

For now, be aware that to avoid further attack from a bully, you will need to learn how to stand your ground and confront the bully instead of fleeing. Once again, if at this stage you are feeling apprehensive about being able to do this, know that this is normal. Remember your apprehension is fear, and fear is good. All I ask is that you sit with this apprehension until you have read to the end of the chapter. By then you will know the Fear Professionals' sixth secret and how to apply it when faced with bullying.

★ WHO USES MIND GAMES?

Who are the common types of people likely to use Mind Games on you? The scary fact is that they can be used by virtually anyone – parents, partners, children, friends, work colleagues, bosses, salespeople, complaining customers, neighbours, even charity workers collecting donations. We all use Mind Games on one another to get what we want.

I remember a single mother who brought in her ten-year-old son for counselling. She had been single for more than seven years and was looking to date again. But whenever she went to go out on a date, her son would throw temper tantrums, even threatening to harm himself. She felt imprisoned in her own home, with her son in control of the key. What was he doing? He was using manipulative Mind Games to prevent his mother from leaving him.

Mind Games can be used by all types of people, regardless of age or gender. If you were to look at yourself honestly (a difficult task for anyone), it's likely that you have used Mind Games to get what you want too. This shows just how often Mind Games are used in everyday situations, and they are not just limited to the people who fit the bullying stereotype.

 FEAR FACT

Mind Games can be used by anyone.

★ THE INTENTION OF MIND GAMES

If Mind Games are commonly used, are practically impossible to ignore and can be used by anyone, what makes them so powerful? Bullying Mind Games are extremely effective because they make you doubt yourself. Once you doubt yourself, it's a hop, skip and a jump away from questioning your own ability and self-worth, and eventually surrendering control over yourself. When this happens, you lose your mental balance, which is like being in a temporary state of psychological emergency. You feel disorientated, unable to think clearly or rationally, your confidence levels plummet and all you can think about is self-preservation.

In the time taken to regain your composure, you will feel confused and lost for words, and will be vulnerable to the bully's attack. This is why it's only when you regain your balance that you can think of great comeback lines.

One of the front-line police officers I interviewed had often witnessed this in the field. 'From my experience, if a person is off balance either physically or mentally, then they have to first regain their balance before they can attack effectively.'

When you lose your mental balance, a bully is able to manipulate you because you will probably respond in one of two predictable ways:

1. Submit to the bully and do nothing: Standing up to a bully seems like too much trouble because of doubts as to whether you'll be able to handle the consequences if you do. It's easier just to keep the peace and do nothing:

★ Ernie gives in to Sam's demands, feeling it is easier to just say yes and avoid the inevitable tantrums.

★ Monique has been verbally harassed by a work colleague for weeks and reasons that if she just keeps ignoring him, the harassment will stop.

2. Lose your temper and attack: The school bully loves nothing more than a victim who bites back. And that is exactly what you do when you lose your temper. A victim who feels powerless to stop a bully often becomes defensive, in desperation, and attacks.

★ The school bully loves stealing Bernard's hat off his head and throwing it around the playground because Bernard gets so irate.

★ Dan cannot take Liz's sly putdowns any longer and swears at her and then storms off. Everyone rushes to Liz's aid, as if she were the victim.

People often mistake the 'lose your temper' approach as the only way of controlling a bully. It's a bit like the 'fight fire with fire' philosophy. In isolated cases it may work but, in the majority, the main problem with losing your temper is running the risk of losing self-control and then doing or saying things you might regret. In Dan's example above, this had the effect of making Liz more sympathetic, probably not his intended outcome.

> **'Egos can be very dangerous because they can make a person ignore their fear.'**
>
> STEVE VAN ZWIETEN

Both of these responses to a bully's Mind Games are unreliable. Why? Because both responses are focused on controlling the situation, instead of one's response to the situation. By that I mean trying to control the bully's behaviour to make them stop. Remember the Fear Professionals' secret from chapter 2 – Control yourself to control a situation. You have no control over bullies, all you have control over is the way you react to them. Keeping control over the way you react is the key to stopping a bully's Mind Games. How to achieve this will be explained later in the chapter. For now, understand that for Mind Games to work, a bully needs you to lose your mental balance so you will focus on trying to control the situation instead of your response to it. In short, a bully needs your cooperation.

 FEAR FACT

A bully wants you to doubt yourself so you will lose your mental balance.

★ A BULLY NEEDS YOUR COOPERATION

For Mind Games to work effectively, a bully needs you, the victim, to cooperate. This is achieved when you conform to a bully's expectations and respond in one of the two ways listed above. But if you fail to cooperate with a bully and respond in ways that are different to these two responses, then their Mind Games will run the risk of not working properly.

If a bully relies on our conforming to ensure that their Mind Games work, why do we choose to cooperate with them in the first place? Many people believe that it's bad manners to be confronting and challenge someone in public, and so won't openly address a bully's Mind Games. Let's consider Anne's situation.

Anne was having dinner in a restaurant when the man next to her lit up a cigarette. She told him politely that he was smoking in a clearly marked non-smoking environment. The smoker responded by protesting loudly, drawing the attention of other diners. Anne felt like a troublemaker and backed down. Why? The smoker's Mind Games now have Anne thinking that she caused this disruption.

To keep the peace we try to ignore the obvious solution of addressing the bully, and instead use the sticks and stones approach, hoping that this will make the bully go away. After exhausting this option and still finding it does not work, the only other alternative we feel we have is losing our temper. Later in this chapter, I will show how Anne could respond using the Fear Professionals' strategy for handling Mind Games. For now, all you need to know is that this strategy is based on not cooperating with the bully.

A front-line police officer recounted his way of not cooperating:

'I was called out to an incident involving a young man who was reported as being violently aggressive. He had already physically assaulted and injured two officers who had tried to restrain him, and was set on making me his third victim. He kept yelling his name out loud and that he was a professional fighter who would take anyone on. I slowly approached him and he shaped up, ready to fight. As I knew his name from his yelling, I outstretched my hand to shake his and, in a very excited voice, said, "Frank! How are you going?" I said it in a very happy mood, like he was a long-lost friend I had not seen for quite some time. This caught him off guard. Puzzled, he naturally put his hand out to shake mine. I was then able to pull his hand toward me, causing him to lose his balance, allowing me to throw him to the ground and restrain him.

'I'm not saying that this approach was the right one because it wasn't guaranteed to work. It was a risk. However, it worked because I did not cooperate with the offender by matching him on his level. Instead I used a different behaviour that he wasn't expecting, which got him off balance first mentally and then physically.'

Choosing to be friendly disrupted the bully's Mind Games by not cooperating with the way the bully expected a victim to behave. Even though arresting violent people may not be part of your daily activities, you can still apply the underlying principle of this officer's technique to your life. Take the angry person at work who gets their way because no one wants to upset them. The work-bully needs you to be quiet and submissive for their Mind Games to function. Imagine if someone stood up to this bully by responding in a different fashion, such as being friendly. Would the bully be initially stunned if they were befriended?

'Backing down can be a good defence if it is not what the bully is expecting.'
DALE RIGGER

★ CONTROL YOURSELF TO CONTROL THE BULLY

To cause the maximum disruption to a bully's Mind Games involves using the Fear Professionals' second secret, Control yourself to control a situation. You cannot control a bully, but you can definitely control your response to a bully, as Steve Van Zwieten explains:

> 'Motivation comes from within; you are the only one that can change yourself. If you say, "That person really got me angry or upset me," this is not true because you allowed yourself to get angry and upset by that person. You can't change other people's behaviour but you can certainly change your behaviour and how you react to them.'

Fear Professionals concentrate on changing their own patterns of behaviour from the way a bully expects a victim to behave. A high-ranking police officer with more than 30 years' experience couldn't stress enough how important this concept was. 'If you can put a bully completely off guard mentally, then they don't know what to do. It disrupts their normal thought pattern of being angry or upset. React differently to what they expect and they'll lose their balance. If you don't follow their rules, the game won't work.'

Whether you follow a bully's rules is usually determined by your self-concept.

★ WHAT TYPE OF HAT ARE YOU WEARING?

The single factor that affects whether we cooperate with a bully's Mind Games is our self-concept – the way we see ourselves. Self-concept is a bit like a hat; it can portray how we feel about ourselves and how we expect others to treat us. If the hat you wear is one that only quiet, non-assertive people would wear, then you will feel compelled to fit this role. Generally we're scared of doing the opposite of what our hat indicates. So strong is the urge to conform to the expectations of your self-concept (helped by others' expectations), that you will even develop reasons not to change. You might decide not to stand up for yourself because people will see you as being aggressive instead of assertive. If your self-concept is one that says you should always keep the peace, then, unless you 'change your hat' to a more assertive one, it will be difficult to change your usual behaviour pattern in response to a bully.

Do you recognise any of these hats?

- **The submissive hat:** 'If I say anything it will only cause trouble.'

- **The aggressive hat:** 'Who does he think he is, putting me down in front of everyone?'

- **The bluffing hat**: 'Just act confident and ignore them so no one will know I'm upset.'

Your self-concept is unique to you. The way we see ourselves is based on our life experiences and personalities. What often determines self-concept is how we develop as individuals, especially from early childhood. Can you relate to any of these experiences?

1. Sarah's father never listened, but just talked at her.

2. Brian's mother always yelled, so he learned not to say or do anything that might upset her.

3. Carmel was teased a lot by other children and grew up believing what they said was true.

4. Simon's parents were dedicated to making him a perfect child, but he felt he could never live up to their expectations.

5. Peter was raised to believe in a God of punishment and judgement, never a God of love. Many of his natural instincts were labelled as those of a 'sinner'.

Life experiences can negatively influence our self-concept and we often accept this without a challenge. It is vital to know how you expect others to treat you so that you can decide whether you want to continue 'wearing this hat'.

What does your sense of self say you can and cannot do? Do others see you in the same way that you do? Is your hat a large one that grabs attention or very small and inconspicuous? What colour is your hat? Is it a fiery red, a sombre black or one that changes to match the colour of those around you?

Once other people get to know your typical behaviour, they treat you in a way that complements this. If they see you as shy, they might overlook you for more outgoing opportunities. If they see you as confident, they might expect you to be the eternal icebreaker. Being aware of the self-concept you project will help you change your usual pattern of behaviour in response to a bully. Doing things differently will break the mould you have set for yourself. We are more flexible and adaptable than we give ourselves credit for. To change your self-concept, change the way you view your personality and what you feel you can and cannot do.

> ### 'Don't play the bully's game; do the opposite of what they expect and use the element of surprise or you'll get beaten every time.'
> TONY WEHBEE

You have learned that one of the most effective ways of neutralising a bully's Mind Games is by not cooperating with their patterns of behaviour. Remember, an unexpected response to a bully will disrupt their Mind Games. Now that you know this, you are ready to learn the Fear Professionals' sixth secret, which stops a bully's Mind Games in their tracks.

Secret 6

NAME THEIR GAME

The sixth secret, Name Their Game, simply means addressing the Mind Game being used on you without cooperating and getting caught up in the bully's 'dance'. It takes practice. If the Mind Game is intended to make you feel guilty, then point that out to the bully: 'Sounds like you're trying to make me feel guilty.' If the Mind Game's intention is for you to submit to the bully's anger then point that out: 'Sounds like you're trying to scare me into doing what you want.' Sound too simple? Naming their game is so potent because it draws the attention away from you and places it back on the bully. There is a saying in law enforcement: 'The person who is explaining themselves is often not the one in control.' The Fear Professionals' technique reverses the roles, forcing bullies to explain themselves.

Many people believe that you have to be stronger than a bully to beat them. But trying to beat the bully with strength, say, in the form of a comeback, can easily be lost at the crucial time. Bullies are expert at playing their game because they play by their own rules. If you try to take a bully head-on, playing by their rules, you will probably lose. If you instead name a bully's game, you are aiming to equal them where they are strongest.

Notice I said 'equal' the bully's strength and not 'defeat' it. Why? When Alan Jones considered game tactics in rugby union, he addressed this notion:

'My view was always to play to the opposition's strength. Take them on where they think they've got supremacy. Neutralise it! I'm not saying that you can overwhelm them if they are obviously very strong, but you can neutralise that strength by matching them where they are strongest. So if we can manage them where their strength is, we will be in front at the end on the scoreboard.'

How can we apply this to the bully? Let's revisit Anne's example in the restaurant, this time using the sixth secret. When the smoker protests loudly, Anne focuses on maintaining control over her reaction and names the bully's game. She leans over and says, 'It sounds like you're trying to bully me into keeping quiet.' The bully, stunned that Anne is not complying, sees everyone watching and doesn't know what to do.

In this example the bully's strength relies heavily on Anne feeling too embarrassed to say anything. Anne responds in a way that the bully is not expecting and she does it without trying to beat the bully outright. Best of all, by not cooperating or getting involved in the Mind Games, Anne overcomes the secrecy that strengthens these games. The moment you bring Mind Games out of hiding and label them with a name, secrecy goes out the window and a bully's power goes with it. All because you have not cooperated. You have not fought the bully with the intention of beating their strength, but with the intention of matching it.

'Always respect your opponent, no matter what it is in.'

JOSH CLEMSHAW

You may feel that the Name Their Game's simplicity is a weakness rather than a strength or that it might be more worthwhile to memorise scathing one-liners so you can beat the bully at his own game, like a lawyer in a Hollywood movie. The problem with this strategy is that it's not reliable – when a bully uses Mind Games, especially in public, your mind tends to go blank and rehearsed comebacks vanish. For this reason alone, when dealing with a bully it is vital to keep things very simple.

★ BUT I WOULD FEEL TOO UNCOMFORTABLE NAMING A BULLY'S GAME

For many people, just thinking about naming a bully's game triggers feelings of discomfort. In Anne's case, she felt uncomfortable that she'd upset the bully. She worried that she would be perceived as aggressive. But this was just what the bully wanted.

Why does a bully want you to feel discomfort in response to their Mind Games? When people feel uncomfortable naming their game, the natural reaction is to doubt that standing up to the bully is the right thing to do. Because we hate this feeling of discomfort so much, we will take the easiest and quickest solution to stop feeling it. That solution usually involves backing down and keeping the peace. The more discomfort a bully can make you experience, the greater the chance of your backing down.

Bullies capitalise on the fact that their victims hate feeling discomfort. Earlier in the chapter you learned that the intention of a bully's Mind Games is to make you doubt yourself so you will lose your mental balance. Any discomfort you feel only speeds up the process of losing mental balance. It's like throwing petrol on a fire. So what can you do to get rid of this discomfort?

Just like fear, the discomfort associated with naming a bully's game is normal and, therefore, something that cannot be removed completely. It can, however, like fear, be managed. The best way to manage the momentary discomfort is to accept it as normal. It shows that you have stepped out of a comfort zone by doing two things:

1. Changing your self-concept from 'submissive' to 'assertive'

2. Avoiding cooperating with the bully.

FEAR FACT

It is normal to feel momentary discomfort when naming a bully's game.

Accepting the momentary discomfort can be used to your advantage. If you feel discomfort by naming the bully's game, it means you are no longer cooperating with the bully. You have stepped out of your comfort zone by responding in a way the bully was not expecting. Well done! The more times you use the Fear Professionals' technique, the less chance the bully will have to use your discomfort to disrupt your mental balance.

FEAR FACT

Naming Mind Games draws attention to the bully's behaviour.

★ BE PREPARED FOR A BULLY TO COUNTER YOU

Let's say you've harnessed your fear and stood up to the bully by naming their game. As the discomfort sets in, your initial reaction is to get rid of this feeling by backing down. You remain strong, though, and remind yourself that the discomfort is both normal and positive. You are just starting to feel in control when suddenly the bully defends himself with his own comeback. This shoots your discomfort levels up and your confidence levels down. What now?

When bullies realise you're not cooperating, they try to increase the discomfort so you will back down and cooperate. Take the example of Brad. He tells a group of his friends that he's taking up ballroom dancing. Most of them are supportive but one says, 'With your weight, I pity the poor person whose feet you step on.' Brad does not cooperate and instead responds with, 'With a putdown like that, who needs enemies?' This places the spotlight back on the bully. He responds with, 'Don't take things so seriously, Brad, I was only joking.' The bully has just increased both the intensity of discomfort and the likelihood of Brad losing his mental balance.

It is during these initial moments of discomfort after the bully's counter that it is so important to resist cooperating. Apply the same strategy that you used when initially naming the bully's game. Acknowledge your discomfort as both normal and positive and stand your ground again. Brad does this by saying, 'We all love a joke, but it sounded like you were trying to put me down.' Now Brad has done two things: he has kept his mental balance and publicly exposed the bully's games by not cooperating.

The bully now has a choice – either to get upset and back down or to try to counter Brad again. For Brad, countering the bully just the once will usually be enough. Even if the bully does try to retaliate again, Brad has publicly shown that he can match the bully's strength in this situation and need not do any more. You may be thinking that this hardly seems like a victory for Brad. But remember that the aim is not to defeat the bully but to match them where they are strongest. By doing so you are not dancing the bully's dance, making you a far less suitable dance partner for the future. A bully needs a victim to cooperate by either backing down or losing their temper, and Brad has done neither.

FEAR FACT

If a bully counters you, stand your ground by continuing to name their game.

When naming any bully's game, concentrate on controlling your reaction to control the situation. The discomfort you might feel is from changing your self-concept from 'victimised' to 'assertive'.

★ HOW TO APPLY NAMING MIND GAMES IN YOUR LIFE

Let's go through some scenarios. We won't list all the different types of Mind Games as it's outside the scope of this book. (If you want to pursue this area, I recommend *Coping with difficult people* by Dr Robert Bramson.) The important thing is to familiarise yourself with the process of naming a bully's game.

To easily identify a bully's Mind Game, just notice how it makes you feel. If, in response to a bully's Mind Games, you feel guilt, fear, anger, hopelessness or even discomfort, then deflect this to the bully. Naming Mind Games can be done any way you see fit, just as long as the Mind Game is named and brought out of hiding.

BULLY: 'We went without so you could get a good education, and this is how you repay us?'

RESPONSE: 'Are you are trying to make me feel guilty for not doing what you want?'

BULLY: (cold silence – the silent treatment)

RESPONSE: 'Sounds like you're trying to punish me by not talking' OR
'Are you trying to make me feel uncomfortable by not talking?'

BULLY: 'If you really loved me you would do it.'

RESPONSE: 'Sounds like you're trying to make me feel uncomfortable because I won't do what you want.'

Notice that in these responses, deflecting discomfort (which is a Mind Game's main aim, after all) works extremely well. This response can be used in almost any situation.

★ HAVING A STRONG REASON HELPS YOU NAME THEIR GAME

Do you find it difficult to concentrate with distractions around you? Naming a bully's Mind Games is no different. A bully will try to distract you so you're unable to name their game. Mind Games can be temporarily disorientating but, if you have trouble remaining mentally grounded, there is a technique to help you. Using a strong reason to face a fearful situation (as outlined in chapter 4) will help you maintain your mental balance so you can name a bully's game.

★ CONSIDER THE BULLY'S POSSIBLE MOTIVES

Generally people won't use Mind Games on others unless they have a strong reason. 'The loud ones are the ones that have a point to prove,' Steve Van Zwieten explained, 'maybe to their girlfriends, mates or even themselves.'

Take the example of Barry, the workplace bully. During his childhood, Barry was often picked on and he grew up believing he was weaker than everyone else. Now, to show he isn't weak, Barry stands up to people he sees as potential threats, even when they haven't done anything to upset him.

'From my experience, people don't attack unless there is a reason.'

MARK ZABEL

Barry was just trying to prove his worth. What your bully is trying to prove will suggest their reason for using Mind Games. Keep in mind that you can only assume what a bully's reason is. Second-guessing what is fuelling the bully's behaviour will help motivate you in finding your own reasons for not playing their game. Take the example of the mother who says to her daughter, 'Jennifer, if you marry Tom, then I'll disown you.' Jennifer surmises that Tom reminds her mother of her ex-husband (Jennifer's father). This assumption helps Jennifer to stand her ground and maintain mental balance. She has taken the focus off herself and placed it back on her mother's presumed motives.

It doesn't matter whether you guess the bully's reason correctly or not. The aim of finding a possible reason for the bully's behaviour is to keep your guard up against them. This in turn helps with your mental balance. Now your attention will be on identifying the bully's inadequacies instead of being tricked into thinking you are the cause of the problem.

Here is a list of some of the reasons that may motivate a bully to play Mind Games on you:

- The bully is trying to boost his self-esteem by lowering yours.

- The bully wants to be seen to have control.

- The bully desperately craves attention and uses other people's misfortunes to get it.

Knowing that a bully needs a reason to use Mind Games is important in keeping your concentration focused. When being attacked by Mind Games ask yourself, 'What is this bully trying to gain by using Mind Games on me?' Remember, a bully's Mind Games can only work if you play their game. Focusing on their reason to use Mind Games gives a secret insight into the bully's mindset and puts the spotlight back on them.

★ A FINAL NOTE ON NAMING A BULLY'S GAME

If someone is using Mind Games on you, then recognise your own reaction and change it by naming their game. It is likely that you will feel fear at first. But what you stand to gain is well and truly worth it. You will have increased confidence as you'll be able to say no to those people who try to manipulate you for their own reasons. You may also have more free time to do your own things, not those that others manipulate you to do.

If you assess the potential risks of a situation and you still feel it's too risky to stand up to a bully and name their game, try applying the Fear Professionals' secret from chapter 5 and share your fear with others who can help. Let's think of it in practical terms: Toby dreaded going to school because the school bully physically threatened him daily. After assessing the risks (using Positive Pessimism), Toby knew that naming the bully's game to his face would only get him beaten up. So Toby shared his fear and named the bully's game, not to the bully, but to a teacher. The bully's Mind Games were still brought out of hiding and the teacher reported the bullying.

Most of us don't have teachers we can call on for support. Yet with a little creative thinking and research, we can find people in the community to ask for help. Who could you name a bully's game to in order to get help? In the earlier example of Monique being verbally harassed by a colleague, she could take her complaint to a manager, a union representative, fellow workmates or even a government anti-discrimination body. Sharing your fear is powerful in naming a bully's game because Mind Games rely on secrecy. The more people who openly know about you being bullied, the more the Mind Games are brought out of hiding. Remember it is very hard for a bully to keep using Mind Games if their mask is lifted.

EXERCISE

To prepare for naming a bully's games, practise 'wearing a different hat' by doing small things that would not conform with your typical behaviour. Go to a movie that you would not normally see, treat yourself to something that you would not normally buy, eat a dish that you've never tried before. See how it feels.

CHAPTER SUMMARY

IN THIS CHAPTER YOU LEARNED:

1. Mind Games are emotional tricks a bully uses to manipulate you into feeling guilty, scared, humiliated, uncomfortable or defensive, so that you will do what the bully wants.

2. Mind Games are almost impossible to ignore and can be used by anyone.

3. The Fear Professionals' sixth secret – *Name Their Game*.

4. Standing up to a bully requires two stages:

    a) Changing your usual response so as not to cooperate.

    b) Accepting the momentary discomfort for doing so.

CHAPTER 7

Welcome fearful thoughts

'It's the lead-up to it, the thinking time that causes the fear.'

Wayne Bennett, former coach of the Australian Rugby League team

'Preparation is everything. A player has to even practise how they will think before a game. Because it's here, before the game, that fear brings so many players undone.'

Michael Broadbridge, former assistant coach for the Collingwood football club

Have you ever been really keen to leave your comfort zone to try something new, only to become immobilised by thoughts of the worst? Like most people, chances are you have. Mark Taylor certainly has. And he would pass on some well-worn advice to younger cricketers before the match:

> 'As you're walking out there to the centre of the field, you may have distracting thoughts saying, "I'm nervous and everyone else isn't!" That's not true. You can just about rest assured that the bowler is nervous, hoping he bowls the ball well and doesn't get hit for six. The wicket-keeper is fearful of not catching the ball, and the umpire is fearful of not being able to make the right decision under pressure.
>
> 'The key is to know that distracting thoughts brought on by fear are normal and not to be obsessed by them. Obviously everyone wants to be as cool as a cucumber in a stressful situation, free of fear and distractions. But I think being nervous helps you be sharp, keeps you on your game, you're not asleep out there, and you're ready to go. So when you think about fear and treat it like this, then it becomes very powerful.'

Fear Professionals know that they cannot permanently stop distracting thoughts, especially when facing a fearful situation. The distracting thoughts can be words or images that pop into your head uninvited, telling you that you will not be able to cope with the situation. They can cause a lowering of self-confidence and avoidance of certain situations. And often the harder we try to ignore distracting thoughts, the firmer their foothold becomes.

Before I learned to harness my fear, I would get all excited about trying new things – moving house, getting a new hairstyle, changing jobs, even repairing something around the house. But the more I thought about facing these new challenges, the more the images of failure and embarrassment would pop into my mind. These negative thoughts drained my confidence to the point of fearing and, ultimately, resisting the new challenge.

Managing these thoughts is the biggest obstacle for many of us when we try to step out of a comfort zone. In this chapter you will discover what fuels distracting thoughts and why they are so difficult to drive from your mind. You will learn what Fear Professionals tell themselves prior to facing a fearful situation to control their distracting thoughts. You will also learn why Fear Professionals force themselves to concentrate on their distracting thoughts when preparing to face a fearful situation, and how different this strategy is compared with the common 'Just ignore it' solution. Finally, you will be introduced to the Fear Professionals' seventh secret, their unconventional way of handling distracting thoughts.

Whether taming lions or flying planes, if a Fear Professional doesn't manage distracting thoughts correctly, these thoughts can become dangerous. Fear Professionals can't afford to let their concentration stray from the job at hand. You may think that Fear Professionals should not be vulnerable to distracting thoughts. After all, they are professionals, the elite in their field; they should be able to block out all distractions, right? WRONG!

MYTH 7

WHEN LEAVING A COMFORT ZONE, SUCCESSFUL PEOPLE DON'T SUFFER FROM DISTRACTING THOUGHTS.

Fear Professionals are human too. When they prepare to leave a comfort zone and face a fearful situation, they are plagued by distracting thoughts. Fear Professionals acknowledge that distracting thoughts cannot be done away with permanently, but only managed. Research shows that when people try to suppress their thoughts, their efforts will only be partly successful at best. In some cases these attempts may create a vulnerability to the unhelpful thought, allowing it to resurge. Ironically, efforts to suppress undesired thoughts can create an unwanted obsession with those thoughts.

**'Generally a fighter will be more concerned
or preoccupied with losing than winning.'**

LES WILSON

It is a misconception that successful people, when preparing to step out of a comfort zone, are able to block out all distracting thoughts all the time. This false belief is damaging for two reasons. Firstly, it puts you at risk of feeling abnormal for experiencing distracting thoughts. Secondly, these feelings will be compounded when you're unable to drive the distracting thoughts from your mind. Fear Professionals know that unhelpful thoughts surrounding a fearful situation are nearly impossible to drive from your mind. So instead of trying to get rid of them, Fear Professionals focus on how to best live with them.

Jim Cassidy explained how he manages this:

'In racing there are more downs than there are ups. It's hard because in racing you've got a lot of people that you have to keep happy: the public, the owners, the trainers, the stewards. In our game you've got to be winning to keep people happy, which can play havoc on your mind. But then I learned you have to be realistic;

you can't be winning all the time and, therefore, you can't be the apple of everyone's eye. I think knowing this and accepting that things may not always be smooth is what allows me to handle the distracting thoughts and focus on the job at hand.'

Jim Cassidy wins the Cox plate. (Photo: Bruno Cannatelli – Ultimate Racing Photos)

Often the distracting thoughts follow you into the fearful situation, past the preparation stage. 'When my engines failed and I nearly crashed in the ocean, I worked out why a lot of pilots do crash, because the fear is so intense.' Gaby Kennard said. 'Panic gets the better of people when things go wrong. The trouble is your brain tends to freeze when you're in a terrifying situation and I knew that if I panicked, then I'd be dead. So I had to say to myself, "I want to live, therefore I'm going to have to think." It got down to living or dying and it was so absolutely terrifying; telling myself to think clearly was what saved me.'

Now Gaby was entitled to have distracting thoughts in this situation. After all, she was about to crash into the ocean. But just because you don't face situations like the Fear Professionals does not mean that managing distractions is beyond you. We all experience distracting thoughts before potentially stressful situations. Here are some everyday examples that you may relate to:

- Barry is running late for work and can't concentrate on driving due to thoughts of his boss's reaction.

- The night before her speech, Susan is so stressed that she cannot get to sleep.

- In the dentist's waiting room, Sam has trouble taking in the magazine he's reading because he's concerned he has cavities.

If you can relate to having any of these distracting thoughts, rest assured you are not alone. Why would you not have distracting thoughts if you're about to attempt something new? Whether leaving your comfort zone involves getting a dead rat out of your house, going to the gym to lose weight, going to the movies by yourself, committing to a mortgage or being left to cook for the family when you don't know how, your distracting thoughts are a normal response to fear. However, like fear, if these distracting thoughts are not managed correctly, they run the risk of sabotaging your confidence.

So what can you do? The first step in taking control of distracting thoughts is to acknowledge and accept them as normal. That's right! Simply accepting them as commonplace gives back confidence and ultimately allows you to control them. Jim Cassidy uses this to his advantage: 'It's the riders who get distracted by the crowd and stop concentrating on what they are doing at the time who are most likely to cause accidents. Sure, there are always going to be distractions, especially the one of a large crowd. Therefore it's very important to accept the distractions as normal so you can free your mind to concentrate fully on riding.'

Remember, it is normal to feel fear in response to new challenges and with these new challenges come distracting thoughts.

FEAR FACT

It is normal to have distracting thoughts prior to facing a fearful situation.

When you accept your distracting thoughts, you will be in a stronger position to deal with them. The next step is to know how your thoughts are influencing the way you behave.

★ HOW INFLUENTIAL ARE YOUR THOUGHTS?

Psychologists claim the person you will talk to the most in life is yourself. These internal conversations occur through our thoughts and are referred to by psychologists as self-talk. The average person, when engaged in self-talk, generally 'speaks' over 500 words a minute. This equates to half the text in this book in less than an hour.

> **'The way you talk to yourself is the way you react.'**
>
> JOSH CLEMSHAW

Now with all this talking, or thoughts, racing around in your head, it is very easy to lose confidence in yourself when thoughts become negative. When you're unaware of your thoughts, it is easy for them to become unhelpful. When your thoughts become negative, they can have a domino effect, influencing your feelings and ultimately your actions. Imagine the following scenario where you are introduced to someone for the first time. See if you can relate to any of these unhelpful distracting thoughts during the introduction process:

- What is this new person thinking of me? How am I coming across?

- Am I doing anything unusual, awkward or embarrassing?

- Was my handshake too firm? Were my hands sweaty?

- What on earth will we talk about once the introduction is over?

- I can't remember their name – what if I have to introduce them to somebody?

Have you had any of these potentially debilitating thoughts? If you're like most of us, you probably have. But why should you not, especially if you consider the person important or influential?

The way you talk to yourself when you experience fear can increase self-esteem and quality of life. But it's a skill few of us have learned. At school we are taught how to think for adding numbers and spelling. We are even taught how other people thought throughout history, though seldom are we taught how to control our own thoughts. Remember the most important person you will ever communicate with in life is you. This is especially true when preparing to face a fearful situation.

> **'The most important part of handling any dangerous situation is communication, especially the communication you have with yourself.'**
> FRONT-LINE POLICE OFFICER

The reason most people struggle with distracting thoughts is that they are not fully aware of them. So this is the first step. What are your thoughts when you feel fear, such as in the introduction example above? Do your thoughts motivate you to face new challenges with confidence or encourage you to avoid them until another time? Are your thoughts positive and motivating or negative and self-defeating?

Studies show that most people's thoughts are inclined to be more negative than positive. The chance of your having positive thoughts all the time are, therefore, comparable to winning a lottery.

But the picture is not all bleak. Even if we are more inclined to have negative distracting thoughts than positive ones, this is all the more reason to keep track of them so that they can be controlled and not the other way around. Get to know your negative distracting thoughts in detail. The best way to do this is to keep a written record of them. Try this simple experiment: for the next three days, keep a diary of your thoughts. Write down the things you tell yourself and the impact these thoughts have on your motivation levels. If you avoid a certain situation, such as visiting relatives, making a difficult phone call, or complaining about a meal at a restaurant, check to see what your thoughts are. Here is a brief example to show how easy it is to keep track of your thoughts:

Situation	Distracting thought	Result
Sitting a driver's licence test	What if I fail?	You begin to panic, you can't concentrate and your mind goes blank
Preparing to say no to a request	But if I say no, people will think I'm mean	You give in to the request
Going by yourself on an overseas trip	I won't know anyone and people will think I'm strange for being by myself	You stay at home

Once again, being mindful of your distracting thoughts is vital for gaining control over yourself. Using a diary like this will help you identify them. From here, you can concentrate on uncovering what they are and in which situations they occur.

'Fear keeps your mind sharp and helps prevent thinking about taking short cuts.'

STEPHEN GALL

Now it's time to have some fun by making your distracting thoughts jump through the same hoops they've been making you jump through. To achieve this you will need to take your distracting thoughts and apply the Fear Professionals' seventh secret to them.

Secret 7

DISTORT YOUR DISTRACTING THOUGHT

What does this actually mean? To distort a distracting thought you need to examine it from different angles, angles you may not have used before. These new perspectives involve questioning the truthfulness of your unhelpful thoughts. One of the best ways Fear Professionals do this is to deliberately focus on their unhelpful thoughts. This may seem rather odd, especially when common sense would suggest the opposite. But Fear Professionals are able to take control of distracting thoughts by lowering their guard to them. In the same way Fear Professionals welcome fear, they welcome distracting thoughts.

This is a powerful technique, one that neither the Fear Professionals nor I can claim credit for. This mind-control technique, based on Eastern philosophy and adopted by Western therapists to meet our fast-paced lifestyles, is called mindfulness.

★ WHAT IS MINDFULNESS?

Mindfulness is observing without passing judgment. It works by sitting back and just noticing the distracting thoughts that come into your mind without reacting to them. When you remember your first kiss, that is your memory at work. But when you become aware of the effect that remembering your first kiss is having on you, that is mindfulness.

Mindfulness lives in the present by observing the thoughts that are going through your mind right now. It's similar to having an ant crawl up your leg and, instead of trying to flick it off, you just sit back without reacting and notice how it feels.

Mindfulness is based on a form of meditation, so it acts as 'time out' for the mind, while physically engaged in normal activity. To get the feel of observing your thoughts without reacting to them, try an exercise that can be done in your daily routine. Let's use the example of drinking a glass of water. The usual approach would be to grab the glass and drink the water while thinking about other things – What will I wear on the weekend? How will I pay my overdue car insurance bill? Did I leave the iron on at home? – the usual multitude of distracting thoughts. For this mindfulness exercise, pick up the glass of water but this time notice how it feels in your hand. Is the glass heavy or light? Smooth or rough? As you put the glass to your lips, notice how it feels when the water rushes and fills your mouth. Be aware how the water feels running down the back of your throat and into your stomach. Repeat this same procedure for your next sip. Remember your aim while doing this exercise is to just sit back and observe your thoughts without reacting to them.

> **'Your fear is unique to you. You have got to know your fear and then work with it.'**
>
> CRAIG MORDEY

How did you find the exercise? Were you able to observe the types of thoughts going through your mind without reacting to them? When done properly, mindfulness is a great way to really observe distracting thoughts and identify what impact they are having on you. I recommend applying this mindfulness exercise to your everyday life as often and in as many different situations as possible. Try using it when waiting on the phone, taking the elevator, walking to the toilet (even in the toilet), eating your food, catching a train or even mowing the lawn. This is a basic introduction to mindfulness. If you would like to know more, I recommend the book, *Mindfulness in Plain* English by Henepola Gunaranta.

Why does mindfulness work so well in distorting a distracting thought? Basically, it challenges these thoughts in a way that the thoughts are not expecting. Fear Professionals deliberately overindulge in listening to their distracting thoughts to distort them. This principle is applied at the Cadbury chocolate factory, where the workers are allowed to eat as much chocolate as they want while at work. By being permitted to eat as much as they wanted, the workers were turned off from eating it at all.

You can apply the chocolate factory's strategy to your distracting thoughts. Allow yourself to focus as much as you like on your troublesome thoughts and observe how they behave. Once again, to effectively distort them, you need to give them more attention than they bargained for.

Think of a distracting thought as a picketing protester refusing to leave until their point of view is heard. If you try to push them away, it generally makes the protestor feel more determined. However, if you take the protestor by the hand, sit them down and listen to their concerns, all that pent-up energy fuelling them will dissipate. Like with a protestor, if you think you can pretend to listen to a distracting thought without really giving it your full attention, it will become agitated again and protest even louder than before.

★ YOUR MIND MAY WANDER AND THAT'S OKAY

Keep in mind that these thoughts will try to resist your control. Distracting thoughts encourage your mind to wander so that you will react instead of observe when experiencing fear. How often have you read an article only to realise that you have no idea what it was you just read? When you notice your mind wandering off, simply acknowledge this as normal and observe the distracting thought.

The worst thing you can do is punish yourself for not being able to concentrate – this is what the distracting thought wants and needs. The moment you do this you begin to lose control over yourself.

'When it comes to riding a terrifying wave, I'm telling myself to concentrate on the other aspects of the wave as well, instead of just the size of it.' Layne Beachley explained. 'I concentrate on the things like reading the wave, and riding it well, how I will enter and exit the wave. So I think less about the things that scare me and more about the things that will help and empower me.'

It's important that when you are feeling fear, your distracting thoughts do not make your mind wander from the situation you're facing. You need to be mindful and not just react to the

Layne Beachley – world-champion surfer. (Photo: Billabong Australia)

situation. Dick Smith told me that he looks at the big picture to manage his fear when stepping out of a comfort zone:

> 'Some people constantly think about fear. For me fear is too complex, and I don't think that deeply about such things. I don't go around being obsessed about fear, instead I think about how I will manage my adventures to reduce the risk. If I can reduce the risk then I reduce the fear.'

Dick decides to divert his focus from a sense of hopelessness, which provides control over unhelpful thoughts. Focusing on the big picture allows you to concentrate on your performance (which you have control over) instead of the possible outcome (which you have limited control over). You are still mindful of your distracting thought, just not in a way it wants.

'Use fear on fear, ie you have to be scared when facing a new challenge because if you aren't scared, you will take unnecessary chances and won't get that rush you need to see you through.'

ROD WATERHOUSE

Fear Professionals concentrate on all aspects of their distracting thoughts to distort and minimise the unhelpful thought's power. For distracting thoughts to work against you, they need you to become fixated on only the worst aspect of a potential situation. Standing back and observing all parts of the distracting thought will release you from its hold.

EXERCISE

For the next five minutes, keep track of what you are telling yourself. Notice how these thoughts are making you feel. Go on, put down the book and do it now.

CHAPTER SUMMARY

IN THIS CHAPTER YOU LEARNED:

1. Distracting thoughts are unwelcome conversations we have with ourselves and generally occur when preparing to step out of a comfort zone.

2. Fear Professionals tell themselves it is normal to experience distracting thoughts when preparing to leave a comfort zone. Trying to drive them from your mind only empowers the thoughts to dig in and stay.

3. The first step in managing distracting thoughts is to be aware that they exist.

4. The Fear Professionals' seventh secret – *Distort your distracting thought.*

5. Fear Professionals force themselves to concentrate on their distracting thoughts by using mindfulness – observing the thought without reacting to it.

CHAPTER 8

How to re-face old fears

'Sometimes when you have a major calamity it helps you accelerate the process of breaking free of whatever it is you are trying to escape from.'

Gaby Kennard, first Australian woman to fly solo around the world

'The difference between a novice and a champion is this – the fear of losing is something a champion accepts.'

Jeff Fenech, former triple world boxing champion

Have you ever stepped out of your comfort zone to try something new only to feel as if you have totally humiliated yourself? Did you then vow never to face that or similar situations again? Examples of such situations could be:

- not wanting to repair anything around the home after a DIY disaster

- putting off going back to study because you failed school as a teenager

- not wanting to ask a bank for another loan again after having a request denied

- avoiding relationships altogether after being hurt before

- never wanting to speak up again after being laughed at.

Most people have trouble re-facing a fearful situation that has caused them pain before. Yet we hear story upon story of champions making successful comebacks after past setbacks, and we're led to believe that the process is straightforward. The champion appears to make the transition from failure to triumph in one simple step. The part that isn't mentioned is just how difficult it was for the champion to do. So is it really so easy to re-face old fears that have caused us grief?

'It's normal to feel apprehensive about stepping back in the ring after a loss. If you burn yourself on a hot stove, the next time you look at a stove you are going to have doubts about its safety.'

TONY O'LOUGHLIN

We have all faced fearful situations only to fall short of a successful outcome. Yet Fear Professionals have a unique way of re-facing fears that dramatically increases their chances of success. Fear Professionals know that trying to forget a past failure and move on is not easy, nor is it the best way to handle the fear of failing again.

In this chapter you will learn the impact past failures can have on your courage levels and ultimately your behaviour. These past failures leave what I call 'Fear Wounds': psychological scars that influence whether you re-face a past failure or similar situations. You will learn how Fear Wounds, if not cared for correctly, can act as a ball and chain, and how Fear Professionals care for their Fear Wounds to go back to a past fear. The BIG question, 'Should I re-face a fearful situation that has beaten me?', will be tackled by learning how Fear Professionals decide. Finally you will discover the Fear Professionals' eighth secret. Without it, re-facing a fearful situation will be almost impossible.

★ FEAR WOUNDS

Fear Professionals constantly find themselves in dangerous situations so it's not surprising that they feel hesitant to re-face a situation that inflicted pain. Whether physical, mental or emotional, generally this pain leaves its mark in the form of Fear Wounds. Past hurts that cause Fear Wounds include:

- being rejected by others
- failing a task
- being embarrassed in public
- being physically injured or sick
- losing something you value.

Unlike physical scars, Fear Wounds can't be seen because they are in the form of memories. It is this inability to visually identify Fear Wounds that makes them so difficult to care for. And if not cared for properly, Fear Wounds will cause you to avoid any challenge that is similar to the one that has caused pain and defeat in the past. All of this holds you hostage within your comfort zone.

When I started writing this book, I was amazed that one after another, the Fear Professionals told me how they were affected by past hurts – physically, mentally and emotionally. This challenged my notion that Fear Professionals were impervious to the effects of past failings. After many Fear Wounds, Fear Professionals still found it difficult to re-face past hurts where the situations were similar to the ones that had inflicted pain on them. But Fear Professionals are at such an elite level; surely they deal with their Fear Wounds by just 'getting over them' and forgetting about past setbacks, right? WRONG!

MYTH 8

IT'S BEST TO FORGET YOUR PAST FAILURES AND MOVE ON.

Fear Wounds are not something you can simply forget, they are there to protect you from similar pain being inflicted again. Fear Professionals have learned to care for their Fear Wounds with more than such a bandaid solution. They're not interested in trying to forget their Fear Wounds. Why? Because Fear Wounds, like scars, are with you for the rest of your life. Even though they do fade with time, you never completely get over your Fear Wounds. Instead you learn to live with them by:

1. acknowledging them as normal

2. gradually raising your 'discomfort threshold' so you can sit with your Fear Wounds and not react to them.

Fear Professionals acknowledge their Fear Wounds. This is the cornerstone of their ability to face situations that have previously caused them pain. Once the cause of pain is acknowledged, Fear Professionals are able to focus on increasing their discomfort threshold in response to Fear Wounds. This threshold is the level of psychological discomfort you can handle when recalling memories of past hurts. The longer you can sit with the discomfort, the less these memories of past hurts will affect you. Later in the chapter you will learn more about increasing your discomfort threshold to manage Fear Wounds. But before that can be done, Fear Wounds need to be acknowledged as normal.

One person who knows about setbacks is Jeff Fenech. In 1984 Jeff won an Olympic gold medal for boxing only to have the judges change their minds shortly after. He was awarded a silver medal instead. Seven years later, Jeff was competing for his fourth world title, which would have placed him in the history books if he had won. Many believe he did win yet, to his disappointment, the contest was declared a draw.

'I was brought up with adversity, so I can say that the worst thing that happened to me, spoiling me for a period of my life, was too much success. As great as success is, unless you know how to handle it properly – and no one ever does – you only learn how to handle it from your own mistakes. Sure you can read books on handling success, but unless it happens to you personally, you don't really learn. I learned a lot from my success though I think I learned more from losing.'

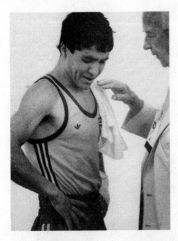

Jeff Fenech in tears after the international jury reversed his winning-bout decision, robbing him of a gold medal at the 1984 Olympics. (Photo: Bruce Howard – courtesy the National Library of Australia)

Jeff would have sustained substantial Fear Wounds after the first bout but he didn't let them cripple him. This allowed him to re-enter the ring, which is a triumph regardless of the official outcome.

Some Fear Wounds are mirrored by actual wounds. For most of us, being bitten by a shark would mean we would never return to the water again, let alone swim with sharks. Yet Valerie Taylor, who has been bitten by sharks more than once, tries not to forget her past mistakes and instead concentrates on them to prevent the mistake recurring.

> 'I got bitten just last March on the foot while filming sharks feeding and I never saw the shark until I felt it tug on my foot. The shark made a simple mistake and mistook the sole of my shoe for a fish. He spat it out smartly.'

Now how did Valerie view this traumatic experience to enable her to get back in the water? She used it to reassess what she'd been doing at the time of the bite:

'Every time I have been bitten by a shark it has been my fault, I have made a mistake. There is a certain way to behave and I had not behaved that way. If you break the rules driving a car you are probably going to have an accident. So if you break the rules working with sharks then there is a possibility you are going to get bitten.'

Ron and Valerie Taylor filming a great white shark. (Photo: Ron and Valerie Taylor)

You may feel that Fear Professionals are entitled to hesitate when re-facing a fearful situation. But you may feel critical of the need for you to focus on past failures. If you do, then don't worry – you're certainly not alone. But successful people aren't able to totally wipe past hurts and failures from their minds just to face a situation similar to the one that has beaten them. The fact is that memories of past failures stay with us as a way of guarding against it happening again.

Joe Bugner admitted:

'My biggest failure came in my very first fight. I was only seventeen and there were many famous actors sitting ringside in the crowd. Instead of keeping my eyes on my opponent, who I was pounding from corner to corner, I took my concentration off the job to look at the film stars. Well, in desperation my opponent pulled out the biggest punch of his career, which put me on my arse and ended the fight. This burned inside of me but later a very famous entrepreneur said to me, "Remember, Joe, the famous Jack Dempsey lost his very first fight."

'I used Jack Dempsey as a kind of a role model and thought, "If he can come back, so can I." Shortly after, I had my next fight and I never looked back from that moment on. I never forgot my first fight, instead I used it as a constant reminder to stay focused.'

If Joe hadn't used his failure, he might have grown complacent and made different mistakes. Whether your Fear Wound is being rejected when asking for something, losing your temper at a meeting or breaking up with a partner, feeling reluctant to re-face these or similar situations is perfectly normal. Can you relate to any of these painful experiences?

- After making a joke at the party and receiving no response, George felt he should not say another word.

- Rod was involved in a minor car accident and now he is hesitant to get back into a car.

- Julian went to a job interview under-prepared and made a fool of himself. Now he refuses to go for any other interviews.

If you can relate to any of these situations or have experienced similar ones of your own, it is highly likely that mismanaged Fear Wounds have lowered your courage levels. If so, you are not 'weak' for being unable to get over past setbacks, but perhaps you didn't know how to care correctly for your Fear Wounds.

'Teaching a player to use fear positively is very important for success.'

MICHAEL BROADBRIDGE

★ HOW DO WE MISMANAGE OUR FEAR WOUNDS?

In the 1960s Dr Martin Seligman, psychologist and author of *Learned Optimism*, made a groundbreaking discovery about human behaviour. Learned helplessness describes the phenomenon of people giving up after pain or failure and then carrying a defeatist mindset into other situations. These people tend to attribute their setbacks to personal flaws instead of situational factors. Seligman's research involved participants answering a 'true or false' computer test. Unbeknown to the participants, the computer tests were designed so that it was impossible to pass. The researchers found that the participants tended to give up in the subsequent tests, expecting to fail again. Due to past setbacks the participants had adopted the learned helplessness approach of thinking 'nothing I do will help'.

How does learned helplessness relate to you and your Fear Wounds? The way you view your Fear Wounds will have a bearing on how you behave in similar situations in the future. If your efforts in life are punished or discouraged long enough and you do not properly care for the Fear Wounds that these situations cause, you risk learning to become helpless.

Take the story of Jed, who was illiterate. Jed felt embarrassed about his inability to read and, every time he tried to learn, his effort met with failure. Jed's wife tried to teach him, but the books she chose were too difficult. Eventually, he just gave up, convinced that it was beyond him. Jed had taught himself to be helpless. It is the way you treat your Fear Wounds that will determine whether you give up or have the strength to re-face a past or similar setback.

Why does failure, or the fear of failure, cause us so much psychological distress? We are encouraged to see defeat as a sign of inadequacy. The message being taught through family and friends, school, sport and entertainment is that winners are rewarded and losers are punished. Consider the 'popular opinion' of:

- the player who misses the goal that could win their team the game
- the student who fails the same test more than once
- the talent scout who decided not to sign the Beatles.

None of these people would traditionally be admired in popular opinion. So it's not surprising that we try to avoid similar failures. We just don't want to feel any pain.

How are we taught to handle the pain from past setbacks? The common misconception is that you should be able to forget the pain from past setbacks by simply 'getting over it'. And if you can't get over it and instead let it influence you, it is likely you will be considered mentally weak. This mindset is everywhere. Even 'professionals' like self-help gurus promote it by claiming that once you've done their course, read their book or mapped out your future goals, getting over past failures will be smooth sailing. Many even use themselves as examples to show how you can rise from the depths of despair by simply getting over poverty or low self-esteem, and become successful, dynamic and rich. However, the advice that many of these gurus often overlook, or leave out altogether, is acknowledging just how difficult it is to get over a past failure or hurt in the first place, especially when your Fear Wound is deep.

Why is it that honestly stating how difficult it can be is generally not talked about? Because we perceive it as being too negative. It's as if admitting that past failures influence us somehow highlights our pessimism or weakness. I regularly see the damaging effects that 'getting over it' has on clients who feel they must forget past failures or hurts. Whether it is the death of a loved one, ending a relationship, having a miscarriage, parents worrying about their children getting in trouble, or losing a job, trying to forget only makes the pain worse. Why? Ignoring Fear Wounds runs the risk of the wound becoming 'infected'.

What do I mean by the Fear Wound becoming infected? Psychological scars that are not treated will steadily lower self-confidence over time. Think of a Fear Wound as a small cut. Even though it's uncomfortable, if the cut is treated with antiseptic and not ignored, it generally heals and scarring is minimal. But if that cut is ignored and becomes infected, it can affect your whole body. The initial small cut ends up consuming your life. Fear Wounds, like small cuts, are normal and a common part of life and, if treated correctly, they heal. If treated incorrectly or ignored, you run the risk of the wound becoming infected, playing havoc with your thoughts, feelings, actions and overall motivation levels.

FEAR FACT

Fear Wounds that are ignored become worse.

How should you best manage Fear Wounds so that they do not stop you from stepping out of your comfort zone? Fear Professionals deal with their Fear Wounds in a simple way. They use the eighth secret.

Secret 8

KNOW YOUR FEAR WOUNDS

Fear Professionals place a lot of emphasis on getting to know their Fear Wounds. This is done by first acknowledging and then respecting their wounds. Knowing your Fear Wounds is like a self-diagnosis. You will learn the treatment later in the chapter. Some benefits you can expect from getting to know your Fear Wounds are:

- preventing self-blame by demystifying why you avoid certain situations.

- being more at peace with past failures or hurts.

- increasing your confidence to face similar situations to those that have caused you pain.

- managing distracting thoughts associated with past hurts.

★ WHAT ARE YOUR FEAR WOUNDS?

The first step in getting to know your Fear Wounds is to recall a past setback, failure or discouragement that continues to cause discomfort when you think of it. A great indicator is if you start cringing and putting yourself down when you think of these situations – 'How could I have been so stupid not to have seen it coming?' or 'I should have known better than to ...'. Here are some common examples:

- Expressing an unpopular opinion only to be publicly humiliated.

- Having your partner end the relationship.

167

- Being misled into purchasing a second-hand item and discovering it is faulty.

- Being talked into doing something dangerous.

Even though cringing and putting yourself down are reliable indicators of Fear Wounds, it's best to choose a situation that was not too traumatic. Start with a small setback and, when you feel more comfortable with the process, move on to bigger situations. Please note, if thinking back on a past situation traumatises you to the point that you cannot function in day-to-day life, then you may need professional assistance to deal with these Fear Wounds.

To find a past situation that may be fostering infected Fear Wounds, take time to reflect. If you are having troubles finding one, then use the Fear Finder from chapter 1 in the same way you used it to become aware of your fear. Take your time. Often the deeper the Fear Wound, the more hidden the situation fuelling it may be.

Once you have your situation in mind, you can start applying the Fear Professionals' concept of getting to know your Fear Wounds. Ask yourself if these wounds influence you to avoid similar situations today. For example, if you had a bad experience trying to return an item to a shop, has this deterred you from returning other items to shops or buying new items? To understand how Fear Wounds affect behaviour, it is vital to understand the relationship Fear Wounds have with Fear Behaviour Patterns.

★ FEAR WOUNDS FUEL FEAR BEHAVIOUR PATTERNS

A great technique Fear Professionals use to increase their discomfort threshold when re-facing a past setback is controlling their Fear Behaviour Patterns. Recall from chapter 2 that a Fear Behaviour Pattern is the automatic response you give when faced with a fearful situation. In a similar way, painful memories sparked by infected Fear Wounds are able to trick your mind into thinking you are actually facing that same situation again. As a result, you will automatically respond expecting pain. Therefore, when you think back on these images of past failure, be aware of what Fear Behaviour Patterns they are triggering. Do you physically cringe, with your jaw tightening? Has your breathing become faster and shallower? Are you sweating or shaking? Can you feel a strange knot forming in the pit of your stomach? What other tension can you notice in your body? To experience these bodily sensations when remembering a past hurt is normal. Sit with these feelings and ride them out. Their intensity will lessen dramatically. This is the best way to control your Fear Behaviour Patterns triggered by Fear Wounds.

Learning to sit with the feelings your Fear Wounds create will allow you to increase your discomfort threshold and eventually master these feelings. Kostya Tszyu gave an unconventional example of this notion:

'In boxing, what makes someone handle fear is discipline over the way they react in training; being able to make themselves train hard. If you want to be really good in boxing, you have to be able to go through sickness at least three times because of training hard. If you can cope with being sick on three different occasions during hard training sessions, then you can become a champion. I have seen people who are sick once because of training hard and never come back, sometimes twice, but not many still stay after being sick three times.'

To you and me, Kostya's example may seem extreme – it's not our idea of how training should be at all. For most of us, if we exercised until we were sick, our fear would strongly discourage us from this type of exercise again (a sensible decision in most circumstances). Kostya explained that to be successful, boxers need to be able to change their patterns of behaviour from avoidance to dealing with discomfort. If boxers were to give up during training when things got tough, they would inadvertently be training themselves to also give up during the real competition. So too, if you choose to give up facing a smaller past setback because of discomfort, you will inadvertently be training yourself to avoid facing larger setbacks in the future. The next time you feel compelled to avoid a situation relating to a past setback or hurt, you can be sure that a Fear Wound is fuelling your behaviour. Sit with this uncomfortable feeling without reacting and it will fade.

★ WHAT IS AN ACCEPTABLE LEVEL OF DISCOMFORT?

It's important to address the question of what is an acceptable level of discomfort to sit with when addressing a Fear Wound. The general rule is that the feelings should not affect your day-to-day living. If you find that revisiting a past hurt is too distressing, leave it and come back when you feel more comfortable or seek professional help from a qualified therapist. This is a very important point. When selecting a past hurt to work on, Fear Professionals choose one that is small and manageable. Otherwise, if the selected past hurt is too traumatic, it could run the risk of destroying the Fear Professional's confidence.

Before we look at techniques that the Fear Professionals use to deal with Fear Wounds, it is worth recapping on the points outlined in getting to know your Fear Wounds:

1. Know the past situation that created your Fear Wound.

2. Understand how your Fear Wound is affecting your current behaviour.

3. Increase your discomfort threshold by sitting with, and not reacting to, your Fear Wound.

The remainder of this chapter will introduce you to five techniques Fear Professionals use to help them re-face fearful situations. These five techniques draw on the information you have learned in the past seven chapters. From the five techniques, use the ones that you feel best suit your current situation. Play around with the techniques and make them your own. Please note that I am not advocating that you should re-face every situation that has previously caused you pain. If your situation is too traumatic to even consider re-facing, then leave it alone and seek professional help.

★ TECHNIQUE 1: RE-FACE FEAR IN YOUR MIND FIRST

Preparation is important before facing a fearful situation. An effective way of preparing to face a past hurt is to first re-face it in your mind. See yourself doing the desired action in your mind's eye before you physically do it. Fear Professionals know that visualising themselves re-facing a past hurt before actually doing it is a potent confidence-building technique. Stephen Gall recommends it to the elite motocross riders who have had an accident on the track:

> 'You have got to prepare yourself in your mind about how to do it correctly after you've had the problem that has given you your fear. First you have to learn to manage that fear in your mind. Then you can plan and prepare yourself better for the next time.'

The key to re-facing a past hurt in your mind is to become aware of the effect the images of the past hurt are having on your body. This can best be achieved by applying mindfulness, from chapter 7, in three simple steps:

1. Imagine stepping out of your body and then floating up and looking down on yourself from a great height.

2. While observing yourself from a second-person position, notice how the discomfort of revisiting a past hurt is affecting your body. Give this discomfort a rating out of ten where one is relaxed and ten is extremely tense.

3. If this discomfort were a colour what would it be?

The more you can dissociate yourself from the discomfort and identify its impact on your body using mindfulness, the less severe the uncomfortable feelings will become. Becoming aware of the Fear Behaviour Patterns these images are triggering will help free your mind from their stranglehold. Once again, if you choose to face a Fear Wound in your mind and it is too painful to visualise, then leave it alone.

★ TECHNIQUE 2: TAKE SMALL STEPS

The main strategy Fear Professionals use to re-face situations that have left wounds is to approach them in manageable steps. You may recall Gaby Kennard's advice from chapter 2: 'I believe that if I approach a fear slowly and carefully, and go a little bit further each day, I will get there.' During her flight around the world, Gaby put this advice into practice when she was close to calling off the whole adventure. Her confidence was rocked when she barely escaped a terrifying experience that nearly took her life:

'When I landed safely after nearly crashing in the ocean due to my engine failing, the fear and trauma to get back in the plane again to finish the trip were incredible. After I finally convinced myself to get back in the plane to continue, when it came time for me to take off, I couldn't. I had this reaction to the trauma and I tried to take off about three times and couldn't do it. I was so trembly and terrified. So I thought, "Well, I don't have to do a twelve-hour flight. How about I halve it and do a six-hour flight?" This seemed possible, which allowed me to take off and once I got up to a decent height, I was okay.'

Once you have the situation in mind that you want to re-face, use Gaby's advice and plan how you can break it down into manageable parts so that you can take smaller steps to achieve your goal. Studies show that public speaking is the greatest fear people have, even greater than dying, so let's use this as an example. Toastmasters, the organisation that promotes public speaking groups, helps new members handle this fear by using small steps. New members will be asked if they want to introduce themselves. Each subsequent occasion that they attend, the duration and complexity of their public speaking is gradually increased. Eventually, the task doesn't seem quite so daunting.

★ TECHNIQUE 3: KNOW WHY YOU WANT TO RE-FACE A PAST HURT

According to the old saying, 'If you fall off the horse, you have to get straight back on it.' In horse racing, with the horses travelling at high speeds, if you fall off it could be fatal. I asked Jim Cassidy why he would get back on a horse after a fall:

'It's the love of my job that would motivate me to get back on after a fall. I love the speed, I love the adrenaline and, most of all, I love winning. I think when I lose this desire to succeed I'll retire and hang my boots up.'

Jim knows that without a reason he would not re-face the fear of getting back on a horse after having a fall. It is important that you apply a similar approach to Jim's when preparing to re-face a past hurt – have a strong reason.

To discover your reason for re-facing a past failure, you need to ask yourself one simple question: What is to be gained by re-facing my fear?

This is a vital question. Remember, if you have faced a fearful situation and now have no intention of, or can see no reason for, re-facing it, then walk away. That's right, unless you have a strong reason, it will be extremely difficult to successfully re-face a past setback. If you're embarrassed about an outburst you made at your social club, your reason to apologise might be that you really enjoy the other members' company. Once again, know the reason why you want to re-face a past hurt or failure.

★ TECHNIQUE 4: HAVE A ROLE MODEL

When preparing to re-face a fearful situation, model yourself on someone you consider courageous. This doesn't have to be someone you know personally. It could be a celebrity or even a fictional character out of a novel. Often just watching or reading about how these people have learned to manage their fear can provide you with valuable support. Stephen Gall explains:

> 'If something has happened where you have lost your confidence or you have a fear of something, then you can visually watch other people do it and learn from them. It can help just knowing that you're the same as them, that they are flesh, blood and bones like you. If they can do it, then so can you.'

Here are some possible role models, all of whom have made successful comebacks from a past setback:

- Winston Churchill was plagued with depression but fought on to defeat the Nazis in World War II.

- Gloria Estefan broke her back in a car accident and was able to make a full recovery to continue her singing and dancing career.

- Anthony Warlow beat cancer and remains one of Australia's top singers.

'You can draw strength from other people's experiences.'
TONY BATTEN

What if you cannot think of a suitable role model who relates to your current situation? Then you need to go looking. Some of the best places to find a role model include:

- books (especially biographies)
- motivational audio tapes
- television interviews/documentaries
- seminars.

'If you are scared about trying something new, you can learn from other people who have been doing it longer than you.'
PAUL ISGRO

When facing a past hurt, ask yourself how your role model would face it if they were in your shoes. Imagine you are about to walk into a room where everyone is already sitting and you know that when you walk in, all eyes will be on you. If your role model is Oprah Winfrey, for example, ask yourself how she would enter the room and what she would say to herself during the process. Then do the same. Act the way you think your role model would if they were in your current situation. This requires a degree of courage and imagination. Remember, when it comes to mustering up the courage to re-face a past hurt, you do not have to act like your old self.

★ TECHNIQUE 5: BELIEVE IN YOURSELF

A common misconception is that to believe in yourself means to be 100 per cent confident of success and, if you feel fear, it indicates you have doubts. Fear Professionals reject this kind of thinking. As you learned in chapter 1, we all feel fear. When it comes to re-facing a past hurt, believing in yourself is about knowing you can handle your Fear Wounds, especially when they try to influence you to run. Believing in yourself is a major factor that fuels courage levels and is vital to ensure a successful outcome. Neville Kennard put it simply when he said, 'Courage is believing in yourself.'

> **'You can have anyone, no matter how famous, tell you that you can do something. But if you don't believe in yourself, then that is a real battle.'**
>
> SHANNAN TAYLOR

When Mark Taylor went through a slump in his cricketing career, some people suggested he was past his prime and should retire. 'I suppose the fear I felt in this instance was thinking,

Mark Taylor in action against South Africa, Adelaide, 1998. (Photo: AAP Image)

"Maybe some of these stories about me are true. Maybe I had lost it. Maybe I wasn't the player I used to be." But I felt inside that I was, and I believed in myself all along.'

A powerful way to believe in yourself is to prepare properly. Alan Jones uses an interesting catchphrase to explain this:

'It's not easy being an athlete and facing the unknown on a regular basis. It can be scary. So that is when you need faith. You must believe. You have to believe and tell yourself that, "If you've done the homework then you'll pass the exam."'

Believing in yourself is easier when you believe you have prepared yourself properly to face a Fear Wound. Go back through these five techniques and apply them in your life wherever and whenever you can. The most important point of all when preparing to re-face a past hurt is to be aware of your Fear Wounds and care for them. Remember, Fear Wounds that are ignored get worse and this will only rob you of your confidence. Jim Cassidy captured the importance of re-facing past hurts: 'There will always be a hurdle there in front of you but, if you don't try to jump it, you'll never get to the other side.'

EXERCISE

Deal with incomplete or unnecessary things in your life, such as clearing out your wardrobe of old clothes or filing incomplete paperwork. Incomplete things will only serve as reminders of failure.

CHAPTER SUMMARY

IN THIS CHAPTER YOU LEARNED:

1. We all make mistakes and are often scared to re-face them, but putting these hurts behind you by ignoring them is difficult if not impossible.

2. Fear Wounds are psychological scars left from past failures or setbacks and, when ignored, get worse.

3. The Fear Professionals' eighth secret – *Know Your Fear Wounds*.

4. A Fear Professional needs a strong reason to re-face a past hurt and if there is no offer of potential gain, they will not face it.

5. When re-facing a past hurt, Fear Professionals use five techniques to manage Fear Wounds.

CHAPTER 9

Your intuition

'Don't ask me how the gut instinct works; if I could explain
it I'd be rich. Just listen to it.'

Police officer

Fear Is Power has focused on control and preparation when dealing with potentially fearful situations, but there are occasions where it pays to listen to your 'gut instinct' or intuition. Metaphysical states vary from person to person and cannot be measured 'scientifically' so it is impossible to determine just where one's intuition stops and fear begins. Nevertheless, experienced Fear Professionals attest again and again to the benefit of attuning oneself to intuition. As this police officer recounted:

'Experienced officers have developed this gut instinct to the point where they can walk into a room and, virtually straight off, pick out the troublemakers. This gut instinct is very reliable, so much so that I have bet my life on it many a time, and the one time I ignored it, it nearly got me and my partner killed.

'We got called to a pub because there was a drunk refusing to leave. When we arrived I had a feeling something was wrong. I ignored it and, instead of at least looking through a window to see if it was safe to enter or if back up would be needed, the two of us proceeded to blindly enter the establishment. As we walked in, 30 angry bikies surrounded us, covering the door so we couldn't escape. It was terrifying, like walking into a lion's den. I knew I had to think quickly or I would end up a cripple or dead. I asked who the leader was and a small guy covered in tattoos stepped forward. I then had a talk with him and basically bluffed my way out by saying there were more officers outside as we were doing routine inspections.

'The thing was, my gut had told me not to go in the pub but I ignored it because it seemed like overreacting. Ignoring my gut instinct nearly got both my partner and I killed. Always listen to that gut instinct.'

Fear Professionals all share the same viewpoint: be attuned to your intuition! They did not have any one particular name that described this internal warning signal. Instead they used a number of different names, some of which you may have heard:

- Intuition
- Gut instinct
- Sixth sense
- A feeling
- Danger alarm

- The vibe
- Little voice in your head
- Alarm bells
- The mind's eye
- Guardian angel

Learning to pay attention to your intuition can alert you to all sorts of dangers. Here are some examples in everyday situations:

- Judy can't help but feel her husband is having an affair long before there is any proof.

- Harold has a feeling he should have his car's engine oil checked. When he does, he finds there was a leak and it was nearly empty.

- Bill suddenly feels compelled to check on his son, just when he is about to explore an electrical socket.

- Esme isn't comfortable with the doctor's diagnosis and gets a second opinion, only to find that the first doctor was wrong.

In this chapter you will learn how the Fear Professionals use a simple technique that enables them to identify and then listen to their intuition.

'It's always good to be a little bit nervous when facing a new challenge.'

ROY ALEXANDER

Fear Professionals pay constant attention to their intuition when making difficult decisions, especially when there is high risk involved. Intuition, they claim, provides insight and gives them the edge to make rapid and effective decisions. Above all, intuition warns the Fear Professionals against danger in situations where logic would suggest there was no obvious risk at all. But surely Fear Professionals prefer to listen to the facts instead of something that can't even be properly defined. After all, if Fear Professionals face dangerous situations on a regular basis, they would ignore hunches and base decisions on rational logic and evidence, right? WRONG!

MYTH 9

IT'S ALWAYS BEST TO TRUST FACTS OVER FEELINGS.

Fear Professionals have such a high regard for intuition that they sometimes place it above rational logic and facts. They know that even though this feeling, or internal warning, is intangible, it is designed to protect. Many people find this concept hard to accept in our 'information age', which places importance on scientific proof, evidence and facts when making decisions. If a person cannot prove that their intuitions, feelings or hunches are right, they are dismissed by others. 'Most people in society no longer use and listen to their intuition, though in our job it is probably the greatest weapon an experienced officer has on their side,' one police officer said. Put simply, it can be an essential survival tool.

Fear Professionals listen to their intuition when making decisions that could mean the difference between success and failure. Because they are often exposed to danger, they may be better equipped to predict potential risks. So if you're not often exposed to life-threatening situations, will your intuition still work for you? The good news is that it will. Yet some people simply do not know how to use it. By understanding the way in which people mismanage their intuition, you will have a distinct advantage in not falling into the same trap.

★ HOW WE MISHANDLE OUR INTUITION

When it comes to decision-making, we are often taught to be analytical. Analyse a problem thoroughly, list all your different options, evaluate these options based on a common set of criteria, determine how important each criterion is, rate each option on the criteria, do the sums and then work out which option has the score that suits your needs. This process is based on logic, which leaves little to chance. It also allows you to justify your decision to others. But it makes no allowances for decisions that cannot be measured, such as those based on feelings communicated by your intuition.

Your intuition is a primal tool our early ancestors would have used. It warns against approaching danger; as long as it saved their lives, our ancestors didn't need any scientific proof. Now, however, we gain security from concrete, scientific answers that can be proven. Therefore, a response based solely on a feeling can be easily overshadowed and replaced by one that can argue its position with logic.

Mary, a client of mine, was very depressed after being the only surviving passenger in a motor-vehicle accident. The driver of the car had been drinking and lost control, crashing into a pole. As a result of the accident, Mary was confined to a wheelchair for the rest of her life. During our discussions, she said she blamed herself for the accident because on that night something was telling her it was not safe to get in the car, but she didn't want to cause trouble and got in anyway. Mary felt that if she had listened to this feeling instead of ignoring it, her friends would still be alive and she would still be walking.

The decision to ignore her intuition is not unique to Mary. It is something we have all done in the past, both Fear Professionals and Fear Novices.

In a (thankfully) light example, I ignored Fear's Voice and have the evidence to prove it — a useless second-hand dishwasher. Apart from the knocking noise it made when switched on, the machine looked fine. When it came time to make the decision whether to buy it, I ignored my intuition screaming at me not to buy it. Why? Because I had three perfectly logical counter-arguments as to why I should buy it:

1. My baby daughter and I had driven too far to go home empty-handed.

2. I wanted to surprise my wife when she came home from holidays (unfortunately the machine surprised both of us).

3. The man who sold it to me lived in an expensive house, drove a Volvo and looked honest.

As a result of ignoring my intuition, I am now the owner of a very expensive doorstop that is collecting dust in the shed.

Why do so many of us ignore our intuition? The main reason is indecision. In times of indecision, you will often feel compelled to go with what is logical or what seems safe on the surface, all in an attempt to relieve the discomfort of indecision. For many people, a decision based on 'the facts' seems like the safest way out.

So how can we distinguish intuition from the facts?

★ WHY FACTS ARE NOT ALWAYS BEST

The biggest problem with basing all decisions on logic instead of feelings is that humans are not robots. We are emotionally driven creatures and not as rational as we would like to believe. Facts may inform us, but feelings motivate us. If you're in any doubt, think of all the cars bought for their image and not their practicality.

The problem with logic as opposed to intuition is that it needs facts to make a decision. But what if there are no facts at hand? You make assumptions.

Assumptions are forgeries of the truth, or *the facts you have when you don't have the facts*. Assumptions seem concrete at the time though they are really just guesses. Take the example of the person who has a bad feeling about accepting a new job (as soon as you have a feeling that cannot be backed up with fact, you suspect it's just your intuition). Because there is no proof anything is wrong, the mind makes assumptions like, 'But the employer has promised you a good wage and it would be great to have more money. Besides, you need a change and you're sick of your old job.'

It's here, when you ignore your feelings and listen to assumptions – no matter how logical – that problems begin. Here are some other examples of how listening to a logical argument (shown in italics) will influence you to ignore your intuition:

- I am not sure if my new boyfriend is right, *but there won't be anyone else out there for me.*

- I know I can't afford this shirt because of all the debt I'm in, *but it's difficult to find clothes that fit me well.*

- I think this pain in my chest is getting worse, *but if I go to hospital and it is nothing, they will think I'm overreacting and I will only be taking up room for people who really need help.*

Even though assumptions seem logical at the time, there is nothing at all factual about them. Assumptions trick you into believing your decision is based on facts.

FEAR FACT

Assumptions are false facts that try to block your intuition.

Ignoring your intuition and thinking everything will be fine is a sure-fire recipe for trouble. How do Fear Professionals accurately identify their intuition and not confuse it with assumptions? They do so by using the ninth secret.

Secret 9

LISTEN TO YOUR INTUITION

The Fear Professionals' ninth secret is easy to use in everyday situations. When you learn how to recognise and trust your intuition, it will give you insight and enable you to make faster and better decisions. It will help in:

- weighing up a stranger's character
- knowing whether to pursue a new idea
- foreseeing problems or dangers before they occur
- knowing when to take a chance in life and step out of a comfort zone.

FEAR FACT

Your intuition will only ever tell you *what* to do, not *why* you should do it.

★ TRUST – THE KEY TO USING YOUR INTUITION

Listening to your intuition is often hard to do, especially in an age where concrete evidence seems a must for effective decision-making. To heed your intuition, trust is required. One of the police officers interviewed gave an interesting insight into the importance of this trust:

> 'I think you can develop your gut instinct. When I first started on the force, a senior officer told me the best weapon I had was my gut instinct and that I should learn to use it. I asked, "How do I learn?" because I had no idea what he meant. Basically he told me when I have to make a tough decision, listen with my gut and not my head. This simple piece of advice took me a while to grasp because it didn't seem logical. At first I wouldn't trust my gut because I didn't believe it could work.
>
> 'After a while I started listening out for my gut and became aware that it did exist. Then whenever my gut tried to tell me something, I would not let my head drown it out with why it couldn't be right. The more I trusted my gut, the more it looked after me. Being able to trust your gut feeling and do as it says is what gives you the edge.'

As the officer explained, he was reluctant to listen to his intuition because trusting it did not seem logical. Trusting logic over intuition is the major stumbling block people face, preventing them from utilising their intuition.

A police officer on his way to a case. (Photo: Mike Combe, NSW Police Public Affairs)

But you're not alone if you find this level of trust difficult to attain. If you have been hurt in the past and have Fear Wounds, it's normal for this to affect your ability to trust again. We are not automatically blessed with trust; it is something we must learn. Erik Erikson, a well-known psychologist, has studied this idea and worked out that trust is the main skill a child learns within its first two years. So if we unlearn it, or never learned it effectively to begin with, we have to relearn it. Even the police officer above had to learn to trust his intuition.

'When I get a feeling that things aren't adding up or things aren't the way they should be, then I know it's my gut talking and I back off and wait for backup.'

FRONT-LINE POLICE OFFICER

If you have not listened to your intuition in the past, why should you suddenly change and trust it now? It is not realistic to expect that you will simply drop all your old beliefs and put total faith in your intuition. Learning to trust takes time and patience. The more you practise identifying and then trusting your intuition, the better you will become at using it.

★ DEVELOPING YOUR INTUITION

The secret to identifying and heeding your intuition is practice. Just like any skill, the better and smarter your practice is, the faster you will develop your ability. Think back to a situation where you had to make a difficult decision, preferably one where you had a feeling that you should have chosen a certain option. When you've found one, ask yourself these questions:

1. What were the cues or patterns that warned you that things were not right with this situation?

2. What sort of feelings did you get in response to this?

3. How did you treat these feelings?

4. Why did you choose the course of action you did?

5. In hindsight, was your intuition right?

How did you go? Were you able to answer the questions effectively? Did you realise that your intuition was trying to communicate with you (even if you ignored it)? Ignoring your intuition is the most common obstacle to developing it. This is especially true when logic is giving you multiple reasons why you should stick with the facts and ignore feelings.

The example of staying in an unhealthy relationship is a situation to which many people can relate. It is also an area that is renowned for people ignoring their intuition, which tells them to leave. Here are the responses a client gave me after he found his girlfriend had cheated on him and left him with a huge debt.

1. What were the cues or patterns that warned you things were not right with the relationship? *She would often come home late and say she was off with friends. She wanted a shared bank account to show our relationship was built on trust. We did not seem to share the same sense of humour. She would not return the favour of asking me if I wanted things such as a drink.*

2. What sort of feelings did you get in response to this? *I had a feeling things were not right, that it was not the relationship for me and to end it.*

3. How did you treat these feelings? *I ignored them by looking at the bright side and focusing on her positives. I thought I was exaggerating, that we were just knocking the rough edges off each other and things would get better.*

4. Why did you choose the course of action you did? *She was my first girlfriend and I didn't think I would be able to find anyone else.*

5. In hindsight, was your intuition right? *Looking back, I felt pretty stupid for not listening to my hunch that things were not right and ending it.*

One of the biggest tests you will face when learning to develop your intuition is listening to it when situations are emotionally charged. This is a very important point to keep in mind. The more emotionally charged the situation is, the more vulnerable you will be to choosing facts over feelings. This is because in these instances, such as the relationship example above, we are more taken by thoughts of what we could lose by leaving the relationship rather than what we could gain.

FEAR FACT

Emotionally charged situations are more likely to block out your intuition.

★ THE ONE-WEEK CHALLENGE

Here is a challenge I put to you. For one week, begin making yourself aware of your intuition by listening out for it. Whenever you have to make a difficult decision, be aware of the process that is going on between logic and your intuition. Can you identify the logical voice giving multiple reasons why you should do as it says? Can you also identify your intuition, which gives just one simple command (often in the form of a feeling) to do something, but with no explanation? Remember your aim is simply to observe the way you respond.

Once you have your situation in mind, answer the following questions:

- What is your logic telling you? (You can spot it by the way it tries to justify its advice.)

- What is your intuition telling you?

Remember, when first listening for your intuition, you are seeking a feeling as much as words. Let's consider an example.

The dry cleaners were about to close for the day and Olivia needed to pick up her suit. But she was already running late to collect her children from school and couldn't decide whether she had time. When she chose to pick up the suit before collecting her children, she had an uneasy feeling in the pit of her stomach, a feeling she could not explain. When Olivia arrived late at the school her kids were in tears, thinking their mother had forgotten them.

Another great sign that your intuition is communicating with you is indecision. Usually when your intuition talks to you, it will make you feel indecisive as a way to prevent the wrong decision from being made. If you hesitate when about to make a decision, cannot find a reason but 'have a feeling', then explore this feeling further.

FEAR FACT

Indecision often signals intuition.

Once you have identified your intuition, trust it. Be daring and do what it says. Trusting your intuition is the key to unlocking its power.

EXERCISE

When you are having trouble deciding between two things, stop using logic. If it were that simple to think it through, you would have already done it. Instead, pay attention to the single command your intuition is telling you to do.

CHAPTER SUMMARY

1. Fear Professionals frequently rely on their intuition when making difficult decisions.

2. Logic relies on reason and proof, whereas one's gut instinct relies on intuitive feelings.

3. Logic will try to block out your intuition by using facts, reason and assumptions.

4. The Fear Professionals' ninth secret – *Listen to your intuition.*

CHAPTER 10

Enjoy the way fear feels

'I have found the best way to manage the physical effects of fear is to treat them as normal.'

Steve Van Zwieten, Corporate Security/Surveillance Director

'I think what helped me control my fear in boxing was that I wasn't scared of the feeling fear caused and just accepted it as normal.'

Joe Bugner, former world heavyweight boxing champion

You finally make the difficult decision to face your scary situation when suddenly you notice the unmistakable physical sensations of fear sweep over you. Your heart starts beating in your throat, palms become sweaty, hands tremble and your concentration becomes distracted. You start to think that other people will surely notice you are not in control of your body because of fear. Now all the techniques you learned from the Fear Professionals, which you had been preparing to use in instances such as this, are at risk of being overshadowed by panic. Even though you try, you feel helpless and cannot get rid of these physical sensations of fear.

How do you view the sensations brought on by your fear? Do you view them as a good thing or as the enemy? Do you wrestle and plead with these feelings to go away and give back ownership of your body? Most people view the physical sensations brought on by fear as destructive. The way you view them will determine how well you apply the Fear Professionals' techniques.

Alan Jones gave some good advice about handling the physical sensations triggered by fear:

> 'You must confront your fears. Everyone has them. The bloke going to work today may fear he might lose his job – he's read about all these people being put off at BHP or AMP and thinks, "That could be me." So he worries. Parents sending their child to school worry, "I hope Jane is going to be alright."
>
> 'All of this is a manifestation of fear. But you have to confront these fears, stare them in the face, and address them. Be Simon and Garfunkel, in 'The Sounds of Silence', walk out into the dark and say, "Hello darkness, my old friend." Everyone hates darkness. How do you overcome the fear of the dark? You confront it; make it your friend. You talk with the darkness – that's what the

lyrics say: "Hello darkness, my old friend, I've come to talk with you again." No one speaks to the dark; most people are terrified of the dark. The lyrics tell us to confront that fear by engaging it. Make fear your friend.'

Befriending fear is a way of taking control of the physical sensations it brings. Seeing fear only as a powerful ally is different from seeing it as a friend. When you see fear as a powerful ally you are accepting only its positive attributes. When you see fear as a friend, you are accepting it for what it is, warts and all. When fear is unconditionally accepted, you can harness its power much more easily.

> **'Fear is very powerful – back a cat into a corner and it's very hard to beat.'**
>
> CRAIG MORDEY

It is here that people fall into the trap of labelling the physical sensations that are brought on by fear as the warts, thereby treating fear as the enemy. This is where Fear Professionals gain their unique courage levels because not only do they accept the physical sensation fear brings, but they also welcome them. That's right, Fear Professionals welcome the physical sensations brought on by fear – those bodily reactions that many of us are terrified of and avoid at all costs.

If you can relate to this terror, then the final ingredient in this book is for you. This final ingredient is learning to be accepting of the physical sensations your fear brings and then actually enjoying them. That's right, enjoy the physical sensations brought on by your fear. Only then will you be able to allow your fear to provide its full potential.

In this last chapter you will be shown how to take this final step toward embracing your fear, by being challenged in a way you were probably not expecting. This chapter ties in and complements all the ideas and concepts you have learned in the previous nine chapters, so you can effectively use them when facing real-life situations and challenges. You will discover the unconventional role that love plays in helping a Fear Professional embrace the physical sensations brought on by their fear. You will also learn why the majority of people choose to do the opposite and hate their fear. With their tenth and final secret, the Fear Professionals will show you how to view the physical sensations brought on by your fear in one of two simple ways. This technique will give your self-esteem a mighty boost, especially at times when you feel that progress in controlling your fear is slipping.

Based on my interviews with Fear Professionals, I have found that fear is a powerful force designed to help in time of need. Now I am taking this one step further to say that Fear Professionals actually enjoy their fear. It's one thing to appreciate the value of fear, but for Fear Professionals to actually enjoy it is going a little too far, right? WRONG!

MYTH 10

YOU SHOULD NEVER LOWER YOUR GUARD TO FEAR.

Many people believe that you must guard against fear at all times, otherwise physical sensations of fear will take over and you will be seen as weak. It is difficult to embrace anything, let alone enjoy it, if you hold it defensively at a distance from yourself. Fear Professionals know that if you keep your guard up, this barrier makes embracing fear difficult, if not impossible. It becomes a high-maintenance defence mechanism, requiring a lot of time and energy to sustain it. Many psychologists, even Sigmund Freud, claim that if you keep up these defence mechanisms against fear, instead of addressing the issues they are guarding, this can lead to all sorts of health problems. Studies have shown that the types of health problems associated with burying issues around fear and anxiety may include high blood pressure, skin irritations, poor mental health and even illnesses such as cancer. Motives for Fear Professionals to lower their guards to fear include conserving time, saving energy and maintaining physical and mental wellbeing.

Gaby Kennard, after her solo flight around the world, said the most important thing to realise when facing a fearful situation is that feelings of discomfort are normal.

> 'You must appreciate that whenever you are uncomfortable while facing a new challenge, you are growing. Instead of hating this uncomfortable feeling of fear, learn to love it because it is a sign of growth. I like the fear in flying because if it wasn't a challenge, the fear wouldn't be there and it wouldn't be very exciting.'

Gaby Kennard saying farewell to family and friends before embarking on her adventure.

Dick Smith agreed: 'There is always going to be a certain amount of fear in my adventures otherwise I wouldn't do it. To me, risk is like the spice of life; it's like a drug, it motivates me to do my adventures.'

'If there wasn't the nerves from the pressure, atmosphere and build-up to the race, it would be pretty dull.'

JIM CASSIDY

Why should you accept these uncomfortable sensations that, in the past, you've tried to get rid of? After all, from your experience, you have probably found these physical sensations to be debilitating and uncontrollable. Can you relate to any of these?

- shortness of breath
- sweaty palms
- thumping pulse
- dry throat

- blushing
- shaking
- tightness in the chest
- perspiring forehead

These physical reactions triggered by fear are often felt by people who suffer from panic attacks. Some psychologists claim that people who suffer from panic attacks do so because they actually become terrified of the physical sensations brought on by fear and overreact to them. When a panic attack hits, the sufferer commonly reacts to these physical sensations by thinking that they are going to die. They become so fixated on these physical sensations that it only makes the sensations worse. Fear Professionals know that trying to resist and block out these physical sensations of fear usually leads to the sensations becoming more intense and uncontrollable.

**'A lot of fighters feel they have to shut off
from their fear, which I think is harmful
because it helps you see the big picture
and understand where you're at.'**

TONY WEHBEE

Even though the physical sensations brought on by fear are normal, the problem occurs when you misinterpret them as trying to cause harm. Always keep in mind that your fear is designed to help you, not harm you. When you work against your fear and try to suppress it, then fear will work against you. Being aware of how easy it is to misinterpret the physical sensations brought on by fear will better equip you to deal successfully with yours.

★ HOW WE MISINTERPRET PHYSICAL SENSATIONS BROUGHT ON BY FEAR

When I tell people about the Fear Professionals' concept of accepting the physical sensations that fear brings, many find it difficult to digest initially. Rarely does a person thank their fear for making them sweat, stutter and shake when facing a scary situation. Instead these physical reactions are interpreted as being harmful and in no way classed as a help. Fear is branded as the culprit that ruins your confidence and self-esteem. It is hardly surprising that people keep their guard up high when dealing with fear so as to avoid further attack and humiliation from the physical feelings it brings.

Defending against fear means you are showing that you do not trust it. As you read in chapter 9, to benefit from Fear's Voice requires trust. In fact, trust is needed for all the fear handling techniques you have learned in the past nine chapters. Without trusting your fear, these techniques will not work.

Take the example of asking your boss for a raise. Prior to facing her manager, Nicole was able to psyche herself up by using some of the many tactics outlined in previous chapters, such as taking into account the risks (chapter 3), being aware of bullying tactics (chapter 6), and preparing herself for distracting thoughts (chapter 7). Then when Nicole begins to walk down the hall to the manager's office, she confidently reminds herself that fear is power. However, once Nicole hears the manager's voice inviting her to come into the office, the physical sensations of fear suddenly turn from power into a wet blanket, sapping her courage levels. As a result, Nicole automatically raises her guard because she associates these physical sensations of fear as the enemy, leeching her of courage. Nicole reasons that if fear were indeed power, she would not be shaking, nor would her heart be racing. In a last-ditch effort to save herself, she tries to ignore her fear. Yet the more Nicole tries to stop these physical reactions from overpowering her, the worse her body reacts to them. It finally gets to the stage that beads of sweat forming on her forehead have turned into bullets. What confidence Nicole has left has been robbed by these physical sensations brought on by her fear. Finally she chokes, her words do not come out properly and she does not get the raise. Nicole resolves that 'embracing' fear is suddenly a dirty word.

In this example, it's likely that everything was done correctly leading up to facing the fearful situation. So what went wrong? The key element left out was accepting the physical sensations brought on by fear as normal. No matter what comfort zone you step out of, you will experience a physical reaction to fear to some degree. The common misconception took hold – that if Nicole raised her guard up to fear she could block out the associated physical sensations. All this achieved was lowered confidence levels and fear was once again branded as the enemy.

What could Nicole have done to control these physical sensations? The Fear Professionals use a simple but unconventional technique to manage such sensations: they enjoy their fear and encourage it to do its worst. What do I mean by this? Fear Professionals actually challenge these symptoms brought on by fear to increase in intensity. If for example, Nicole's heart is beating rapidly, then she would challenge her heart and say, 'Come on, heart, beat faster.' Likewise, if her hands are shaking then she'd challenge them by saying, 'Come on, hands, shake harder. Let's show my boss just how scared I really am.' This simple technique is powerful because it allows you to regain a sense of control over those physical sensations you thought you had no control over.

If the concept of 'enjoy your fear' is not for you, try substituting the word 'respect'. Fear is like the lions in Tony Gasser Jnr's circus act:

Tony Gasser Jnr with his lions. (Photo: Tony Gasser Jnr)

'I didn't have fear as such when I went in the cage; instead I had respect for the lions. I grew up in the circus and was with animals all my life. Even so, when I was with the lions I'd say to myself, "Okay, I know these animals, and I know what they are capable of. Therefore I must show them respect."'

Fear can hurt you as profoundly as the lions, but only if you do not treat it with the right amount of respect.

★ MANAGING THE PHYSICAL SENSATIONS OF FEAR

If you hold your fear away from you in an attempt to make the associated sensations go away, this will rob you of physical and emotional strength. Why does it take more energy to fight the physical sensations of fear by holding them away from you than to embrace them?

Imagine holding a small can of baked beans at arm's length from your body. It will only be a matter of time before your extended arm starts buckling under the weight of the can. Now if this can were held close to your body, considerably less energy would be required, meaning the experience would be far less painful. You can look at accepting the physical sensations brought on by your fear in much the same way. Trying to ignore these sensations is like holding them away from you at arm's length – very draining. Yet accepting them will allow you to hold these physical feelings close to you, requiring a lot less effort.

It takes considerably more effort to shut your fear out than to enjoy it. Without the Fear Professionals' positive outlook on fear, it would be easy to see the physical sensations sparked by fear as an untamed beast, or worse, the enemy. Can you relate to any of the situations below where you might find yourself treating the physical sensations brought on by fear as the enemy, holding them at arm's length?

- Being flooded with feelings of fear just before giving a presentation or speech.
- Noticing a group of strangers you have to walk past and thinking that if they sense you are scared, it could prove dangerous.
- Having a sudden rush of fear and then trying to sound relaxed when an auditor from the Taxation Department calls.
- Feeling nervous about making a poor first impression on your first day at a new job or course.

> **'Anyone who says they don't feel fear is a fool. Fear is a thing that saves you. It turns on the adrenaline rush and primes your body for action.'**
>
> TONY BATTEN

We often believe that the intense physical sensations brought on by fear are abnormal. We expect that we should somehow be able to get rid of these sensations completely, which is setting ourselves up for failure. Fear Professionals know that this expectation will only result in disappointment, so they do more than just accept the sensations. They use the tenth and final secret to manage the physical sensations brought on by fear.

Secret 10

ENJOY YOUR FEAR

Fear can definitely be shaped and channelled for your benefit. Accepting fear as a positive force is a significant step toward harnessing it. Ultimately the idea is to actually enjoy your fear. As we've worked out, fighting fear, or fighting anything for that matter, takes a lot of energy, time and commitment. We cannot keep up the intensity required to fight for long periods of time. This is where enjoying your fear comes into action. Once a person learns to enjoy their fear, they are allowing themselves to have a rest from guarding against it.

'Make fear your friend.'

JUSTIN ROWSELL

Enjoying your fear does not imply that you are helplessly accepting the circumstances. For example, if a person were in a violent situation, then that person would be feeling fear. When they accept their fear resulting from the situation, they are also accepting control over their response to it. Remember from chapter 2, all you can control is your reaction to a situation. This person's fear may empower them to contact police, seek counselling or other forms of supports to change that situation.

Often people in these situations keep telling themselves that things will get better. Instead of accepting and enjoying their fear and listening to what it has to say, many people try to ignore it.

The Fear Professionals' technique of enjoying fear is effective because it helps you to let go of unrealistic expectations about how your fear and its associated physical sensations should behave. By enjoying your fear, you trust its judgement, allowing it to do its job of protecting you.

★ FEAR AS PROTECTOR

Enjoying the physical sensations brought on by fear may sound like a challenge, especially when you've probably viewed them as destructive in the past. You may also be thinking that just 'enjoying your fear' seems vague and directionless. It is for this reason that the Fear Professionals use an added insight to get the most from enjoying their fear. This insight relates to fear's protective nature.

> **'Fear is energising. It makes you think quicker, heightens your senses, and gives added strength.'**
>
> NEIL SONTER

Fear's basic aim is to protect you from danger, and it will protect you in one of two ways. First it warns you about the dangers of facing an unfamiliar or scary situation. Then it motivates you to perform at your best when facing this situation. It achieves this by priming your body to be fully alert. This protection is absolutely crucial to your wellbeing but its signals can easily be misinterpreted. Knowing why your fear makes you experience certain bodily sensations will give you a distinct advantage when trying to manage these feelings. And knowing that it is protecting you will help you love it.

 FEAR FACT

Fear is designed to help you, not harm you.

★ SEE YOUR FEAR AS EXCITEMENT

When fear is harnessed with acceptance it becomes energising and not paralysing. Fear Professionals achieve this by enjoying what they do. This may not be feasible if you are in a terrifying or life-threatening situation. Enjoying your fear applies to fearful situations in which you have placed yourself voluntarily, such as public speaking, competing in sport and pursuing personal goals. When you feel nervous tension building, remember that enjoying your chosen activity gives power. One of the best ways to do this is to smile. Smiling allows your mind to follow your posture – if you lead with actions, your thoughts will follow. Smiling reminds you of why you are there and that you may as well enjoy it.

Alan Jones knows the power of smiling:

> 'Enjoying what you do is a very important thing when dealing with nerves. I always tell athletes to enjoy it. Recently I gave a talk and couldn't get to see my godson play football. I had a whole lot of people around me when I rang him and they couldn't believe that I said, "Now listen, I have one thing that I want you to re-member for the game. Above all else ..." And they thought I was going to say, "Make sure you make your tackles" or whatever.
>
> 'And I said, "You have got to enjoy it. Make sure you've got a smile on your face. The more you enjoy it, the better you'll play."'

Mark Taylor offers similar advice of how he turned his nervous tension into excitement when representing Australia in first-class cricket:

> 'Keep your fear in perspective. I look at cricket as a game, not life or death. At the end of the day's play no

one is going to live or die due to the outcome. You have got to try and keep things in perspective and simply enjoy it. The more you keep your fear in perspective to the situation and just accept and enjoy the feeling fear gives, the better off you'll be. And in the case of cricket, the more you enjoy it, quite often the better you tend to play.'

So when you feel nervous in front of others, see your fear as excitement, motivating you to perform at your best. ENJOY your fear. Treating these physical sensations brought on by fear as an energiser will have a profoundly positive effect.

> **'I have been boxing for over 26 years and I still feel fear, though this fear becomes excitement.'**
>
> KOSTYA TSZYU

 FEAR FACT

Fear is energising, not paralysing.

Seeing your fear as excitement is not always possible or appropriate. To use this technique will depend greatly on the situation you are in at the time. For instance, it would be totally inappropriate to tell an abuse victim to see their fear as excitement. In this case, fear would be viewed as a protector, warning the victim against danger and the need to do something about it.

EXERCISE

Think back to different situations in your life where you have felt fear. Was it appropriate to see fear as energising or was fear best viewed as a protector? Now think of a relatively small situation that you are scared of facing. Before you face your situation, decide how you will see your fear, as a protector or as an energiser. Remember your fear is there to help you so use it to your advantage by enjoying it.

CHAPTER SUMMARY

1. Fear often triggers physical sensations that many people find uncomfortable.

2. Unrealistic expectations of how your fear should behave are best avoided.

3. The Fear Professionals' tenth secret – *Enjoy your fear.*

4. Enjoying your fear ensures that you do not disrupt its role of protecting you.

5. Enjoying your fear can be done by seeing it in one of two ways: as a protector or as an energiser.

CONCLUSION

Fear is power

When giving talks on fear, I am often asked, 'What is the best cure for fear?' which is like asking, 'What is the best move in a game of chess?' The answer I give to this is quite simply, 'NONE!' I hope you have learned from this book that there is no one cure for fear. **Fear is everywhere, you cannot get rid of it permanently.** This was well put by Alan Jones when I asked him how athletes are able to come back and conquer a fear that has previously beaten them:

> 'Just because you overcome fear today doesn't mean to say that it won't return. It's just in a new form. It just has another brand on it; it's there every week. But your capacity to persistently handle it builds a certain confidence within you, which means that in the end you have the ability to marginalise your fear. Hence the fearless tennis player, Pete Sampras, goes for an ace on the second serve; Ian Thorpe swims the first 100 metres of 400 metres in 51.5 seconds.

You have done it so often that fear is marginalised. And that makes it a lot easier.'

★ FEAR PROFESSIONALS' GREATEST INSIGHT

The greatest insight you have to manage your fear is self-awareness. To use any of the Fear Professionals' ten secrets requires awareness of how and why you react to fear. Whether it is the way you react to stepping out of your comfort zone and trying something new or the way you react when a manipulative bully wants you to do something against your will. Knowing how you react is the key. It is only when you know this that you can do something about changing how fear affects your life. **Awareness is the key.**

MEET THE FEAR PROFESSIONALS

 **Layne Beachley**, a six-time world surfing champion (1998–2003), is statistically the greatest female surfer in history. When she won her sixth consecutive world title in December 2003, she became the first surfer in the world, male or female, to do so.

 **Wayne Bennett** was rugby league coach for the Australian Kangaroos (2004–2005), Queensland State of Origin, and the Brisbane Broncos. Formerly a police officer, Wayne is regarded as one of the all-time great rugby league coaches. He has taken the Brisbane Broncos to five premiership wins and overseen as many series wins by the Maroons in State of Origin.

 **Joe Bugner**, world heavyweight boxing champion (1998), was born in Hungary and launched his pro boxing career in London in 1967. He has since been warmly embraced by Australians and claimed as one of our own. Joe earned a reputation for courage and determination in the ring by taking on world champions Muhammad Ali (twice) and Joe Frazier. In 1975 Joe challenged Ali for the world heavyweight title only to lose on points. Then in 1998, at the age of 48, Joe made a spectacular comeback by becoming the WBF heavyweight champion.

Jim 'the Pumper' Cassidy, at 41 years of age, is still rated as one of Australia's top jockeys, despite being born in New Zealand. At the time of writing, he was the only jockey still riding to have won Australian racing's 'big four': the Melbourne Cup (twice), Caulfield Cup, Cox Plate and the Golden Slipper. With 96 first-place wins to his credit, Jim won his first Melbourne Cup in 1983 riding Kiwi. Then in 1997 he won it again riding Might and Power.

Jeff Fenech, triple world boxing champion (1985–1989), captured the hearts of Australians with his sheer determination and bravery, winning fights even when it meant competing with broken hands. In 1984 he represented Australia at the Olympic Games, narrowly missing the gold medal due to a controversial decision. Jeff has received countless accolades and awards for his boxing achievements.

Stephen Gall, five-time Australian motocross champion (1978–1982), is one of the most influential figures in shaping Australian motocross. As well as competing at an elite level in sprint car racing, Stephen writes technical columns in motocross magazines and is hailed as the country's most experienced motocross instructor. He has also founded his own company, which manufactures orthopaedic knee braces to protect riders from knee injuries.

Tony Gasser Jnr was born in Switzerland and migrated to Australia in 1969 with his parents and their family circus, Silver's Circus. At the age of six, Tony was performing trapeze and acrobatic stunts that included scrambling up a pole that was balanced on his father's head to do a handstand at the top. At 15, he started taming lions as one of the circus's main acts and became the world's youngest lion tamer. Tony later replaced his lion act with the dangerous 'Wheel of Death'.

Alan Jones is now a well-known media personality, but in the 1980s he was coach of Australia's national rugby union team, the Wallabies. Under Alan's leadership the Wallabies had victories in 102 matches and won 23 out of 30 Tests. Alan is widely regarded as one of Australia's most gifted coaches and public speakers, having the ability to tap into people's psyches to bring out their best.

Gaby Kennard became the first Australian woman to fly solo around the world in a single-engine plane in 1989. She encountered many challenges during her 99-day, 29,000 nautical-mile journey, including mortgaging her house to raise the funds and facing the possibility of leaving her two young children motherless. It is no surprise then that Gaby's achievements have been hailed as an inspiration to all.

Dick Smith is a businessman, film-maker, explorer and experienced aviator. He has the enviable talent of successfully managing risks to his advantage, an invaluable skill for a man who has broken many world records. His adventures range from flying hot air balloons incredible distances to being the first person to fly solo around the world in a helicopter, and successfully navigating both the North and South Poles.

Mark Taylor was the Australian cricket captain from 1994 to 1999 and is one of Australia's most successful test players and captains. He made his international debut in 1988/9 against the West Indies in Sydney and then, in 1994, was appointed captain of the Australian team. In 1998 Mark equalled Sir Donald Bradman's Australian test batting record of 334 runs (not out) against Pakistan. Mark captained Australia in 50 tests, winning 26, losing 13 and drawing 11. He is now a commentator on Channel Nine.

Ron and Valerie Taylor are the Australian husband and wife team who have been at the forefront of underwater filming since the early 1960s. They have provided footage for many television and film productions, including that of white pointer sharks for the hit movie *Jaws*. The Taylors have developed a name around the world for their ability to capture footage of sharks in their native habitats.

Kostya Tszyu, world boxing champion (1995–1997 and 1998–present), was born in Siberia, Russia and is only one of a handful of boxers to reign as undisputed champion of the world by winning all three belts in his weight division. Kostya moved to Australia in 1992, feeling there were more opportunities for a boxing career than in his homeland. This meant relinquishing the opportunity to represent Russia in the 1992 Olympics, where many felt Kostya was likely to win a gold medal. An ambassador of Australian Amateur boxing, Kostya lives in Sydney with his wife and three children.

Steve Van Zwieten, with more than 26 years' experience in the industry, is one of Australia's leading experts in the field of corporate security and surveillance. As Corporate Security/Surveillance Director for Penrith Panthers Group, and also Senior Regional Vice President of Australasia for the International Security Organization ASIS International, his expert advice is often sought by the media for stories on security and surveillance.

Michael Broadbridge was Collingwood AFL assistant coach from 1999 to 2004.

Alex Buttigieg, known to many as 'The Sharkman', has become a voice for these creatures by lobbying to protect sharks in their natural habitats.

Neville Kennard opened Australia's first self-storage centre in 1973. Kennards is now the largest self-storage company in Australia.

Johnny Lewis is one of Australia's greatest boxing trainers. He has taken three boxers to world-champion success – Jeff Fenech, Jeff Harding and Kostya Tszyu.

Dale Rigger is Director of Entertainment Security.

Mark Zabel is Security officer for Entertainment Security.

Front-line and Special Forces Officers from the NSW Police Department (63 police officers interviewed in total).

FEAR PROFESSIONALS INTERVIEWED from the BOXING COMMUNITY

Boxing has been credited as helping troubled youths stay on the right side of the law. All of the boxing trainers listed here have received countless accolades for their work in teaching respect and discipline through the sport.

Roy Alexander trains both professional and amateur boxers at St Marys, New South Wales.

Tony Batten is a boxing official who oversees the activities of professional boxing in New South Wales. He is the Assistant Project Officer for the NSW Boxing Authority/NSW Sport and Recreation Association.

Paul Briggs became world kickboxing champion at the age of 18 while competing overseas in Asia's Muay Thai kickboxing events. Now a professional boxer, he recently signed to American fight promoter Don King.

Josh Clemshaw is a former Australian middleweight boxing champion.

Renato Cornett, world-title contender in the lightweight division, was also New South Wales light welterweight champion in 1984 and 1985.

David Grainger is a ringside boxing official and NSW Boxing Authority judge.

Paul Isgro, a respected coach, trains both professional and amateur boxers in the Sydney region.

Dr Lou Lewis is both the President of the Australian Amateur Boxing Association and the ringside doctor at many professional and amateur boxing events.

Craig Mordey, the son of the late Bill Mordey, has followed in his father's footsteps as a boxing promoter and journalist.

Tony Mundine Snr, boxing legend and triple Australian boxing champion in the 1960s and 1970s, amassed an impressive record of 80 wins during his career, of which 64 were by knockout. Tony is now a successful boxing coach and trains his son, Anthony Mundine.

Tony O'Loughlin is a boxing coach who trains both professional and amateur boxers and is heavily involved in helping under-privileged youth.

Justin Rowsell was a Commonwealth Games silver medallist in boxing (1990), who later turned to professional boxing. He now focuses on training young amateur boxers.

Neil Sonter is an amateur boxing coach.

Shannan Taylor, a world-title contender, is the current Australian super middleweight champion. He is the former PABA light middleweight champion, OPBF welterweight champion, and Australian light welterweight champion.

Rod Waterhouse is a boxing trainer who works with both professional and amateur boxers.

Troy Waters, a former world-class professional boxer, is the youngest of the three Waters brothers who were trained by their father. Their family story featured on *60 Minutes*.

Tony Wehbee, a contender in the featherweight division, narrowly missed out on winning a world title and, after an amazing career, retired from boxing.

Ray Wheatley is Vice-President of the International Boxing Federation and owner of the boxing magazine *The Fist*.

Les Wilson is Joe Bugner's boxing trainer.

Bill Yearnan is an amateur boxing coach.

RECOMMENDED READING

Bramson, Robert, *Coping with Difficult People*, Dell Books, New York, 1988.

Crum, Thomas, *The Magic of Conflict: Turning a life of work into a work of art*, Simon & Schuster, New York, 1987.

Dodson, William, *The Sharp End: Inside the high risk world of Australia's tactical law enforcers*, Pan Macmillan, Sydney, 2002. (This book gives great insight into Australian Police's special forces units.)

Freud, Sigmund, *The Basic Writings of Sigmund Freud*, The Modern Library, New York, 1938.

Gunaranta, Henepola, *Mindfulness in Plain English*, Wisdom Publications, Somerville, USA, 2002.

Neu, Jerome, *The Cambridge Companion to Freud*, Cambridge University Press, Cambridge, 1991.

Rachman, Stanley, *Anxiety*, Psychology Press, Hove, 1998.

Rapee, Ronald M, *Overcoming Shyness and Social Phobia: A step by step guide*, Rown & Littlefield, New York, 2004.

Seligman, Martin, *Learned Optimism*, Random House, Sydney, 1992.

Skinner, B F, *About Behaviorism*, Penguin Books, London, 1993.

Welchman, Kit, *Erik Erikson: His life, work, and significance*, Open University Press, Philadelphia, 2000.

Biographies on Fear Professionals

Wayne Bennett:
Wayne Bennett: Don't die with the music in you, ABC Books, Sydney, 2002.

Paul Briggs:
Heart Soul Fire: The life of Paul Briggs, HarperCollins, Sydney, 2005.

Jeff Fenech:
Jeff Fenech: I love youse all, Modern Publishing Group, Sydney, 1993.

Gaby Kennard:

Solo Woman, Bantam Books, Sydney, 1990.

Dick Smith:

Solo around the World, Australian Geographic, Sydney, 1992.

Bain, Ike, *The Dick Smith Way*, McGraw-Hill, Sydney, 2002.

Mark Taylor:

Mark Taylor: Time to declare, Ironbark, Sydney, 1999.

A Captain's Year, Ironbark, Sydney, 1997.

Taylor Made, Macmillan, Sydney, 1995.

Ron and Valerie Taylor:

Blue Wilderness, Fourth Day Publishing, San Antonio, 1998.

The Great Shark Suit Experiment: Ron Taylor Film Productions, 1981.

Great Shark Stories, Bantam Books, Sydney, 1978.

Great Shark Writings, Overlook Press, New York, 2000.

www.underwateraustralia.com.au

Kostya Tszyu:

Kostya: My story, ABC Books, Sydney, 2002.

ACKNOWLEDGEMENTS

Writing this book has been the biggest undertaking of my life, aside from becoming a husband and father. At times it has felt like being dumped way out at sea with no sign of land and then being told to swim for shore. Therefore I would like to thank the following people for making this book possible and for helping me find that shore:

First and foremost I'd like to thank Jonathan Dyer, the mastermind who originally edited this book and brought it to life. Thank you, Jonathan, for your unwavering dedication, thoroughness and professionalism.

My wife, Mel, and daughter, Emma, thank you for your loving support, without which this book would never have been possible. We did it, girls!

My agent, Sally Bird, from Calidris Literary Agency, who believed in me and this book and tirelessly worked to find me a publisher.

Rod Morrison from Hardie Grant Books, for believing in the book and giving me this opportunity.

Emma Schwarcz from Hardie Grant, whose professional editing skills have refined the book and taken it to a whole new level.

Gayle Fairall, who generously proofread the manuscript and whose editorial suggestions were invaluable.

Ian Gunn, my brother and best friend, for his creativity and help with the photos.

My parents, Ron and Helen, who have taught me to have the courage to follow a dream, even when it has meant going against conventional and safe thinking.

My parents-in-law, Bruce and Cynthya, for their support, enthusiasm and love.

My brother Mick and his family, Leanne, Ben, Jade and Mitchell, for their support.

My sister Kazz and her family, Adrian and Zack, for their belief in me.

Ron and Dee Karney, who took me under their wing and helped me find my way in life when I was going through difficult times.

Ken and Dale Fields, for their great advice and insight.

David Thorold, my uncle in New Guinea, for his continued support.

Marie Thorold, for always lending a listening ear. Your life story would make a fascinating book.

Chris Miller, who spent hours sharing his wealth of knowledge with me and helping to provide direction to the book.

Keith Morrison, for sharing his knowledge, stories and amazing memory.

Nick Higgins; Bob Gallager; the staff at Billabong, especially Bruce Lee, Luke Jeffrey, and Mike Perry; John Fordham from the Fordham Company; Tony Durkin from Ergon Energy Brisbane Broncos; The NSW Police Department; and Scott Chamberlain from Penrith Panthers.

And all the staff at my work, Hawkesbury District Health Service, for their support and belief in the book – thank you.

I would also like to thank the following people for generously allowing me to use their photos in this book:

Kylie from Handprint Photography
　　　　(www.handprint.net.au)
Steve Hart Photographics
　　　　(hartphoto@bigpond.com.au)

Bruno Cannatelli from Ultimate Racing Photos
    (brunoc@cannatelli.com.au)
Sheri Forbes (photo of Gaby Kennard with ground crew)
The Fordham Company (Mark Taylor portrait)
Mark Austin (photo of Stephen Gall racing motocross)
Mike Combe (NSW Police Public Affairs branch)
Billabong Australia (Layne Beachley portrait)
Alan Jones
Dick Smith
Tony Gasser Jnr
Ron and Valerie Taylor